Mary Beres
17 Sharon Ave
Welland ON L3C 4M8

S0-ENV-545

Aqueduct
MERRITTSVILLE
and
Welland

A HISTORY OF THE CITY OF WELLAND

The Beginning Years
by William H. Lewis

Published by:
    A.M.W. Publications,
    25 Home Street,
    Welland, Ontario, Canada L3C 2E8

Copyright © A.M.W Publications.
All rights reserved.

First printing, October 1997.
Second printing, November 1997.
Third printing, April 1998.
Fourth printing, November 2000.
Fifth printing, March 2001.
Sixth printing, July 2003.

Text, cover design, graphics and layout created by:
    Kristian Bogner Photography + Graphics,
    28 West Main Street,
    Welland, Ontario L3C 4Z6

Printed and bound in Canada by:
    Welland Printing,
    115 Division Street,
    Welland, Ontario L3B 3Z8

ISBN 0-9682743-0-7

The publication of
Aqueduct, Merrittsville, and Welland
is proudly sponsored by

Canadian Tire Acceptance Limited,

E.S. Fox Ltd.,

and

Lewis & Krall Pharmacy Limited.

CANADIAN TIRE ACCEPTANCE LIMITED
COMMUNITY PEOPLE,
COMMUNITY PRIDE.

Canadian Tire Acceptance Limited was established on East Main Street in Welland in 1961.

E.S. Fox Ltd was established on Thorold Road in Welland in 1934.

lewis & krall
A friend you can trust
I.D.A.

Lewis & Krall Pharmacy Limited is the successor to the Joseph Dilworth Drug Company, which was established on West Main Street in Welland in 1900.

In Flanders fields

In Flanders fields the poppies blow
Between the crosses, row on row,
That mark our place; and in the sky
The larks, still bravely singing, fly
Scarce heard amid the guns below.

We are the Dead. Short days ago
We lived, felt dawn, saw sunset glow,
Loved , and were loved, and now we lie
In Flanders fields.

Take up our quarrel with the foe:
To you from failing hands we throw
The torch; be yours to hold it high.
If ye break faith with us who die
We shall not sleep, though poppies grow
In Flanders fields.

JOHN MCCRAE
(NC)

ves time-honoured traditio

brance Day, the Royal Canadi-
s asking all Canadians to
ce for two minutes at 11:00
n is asking people to stop
are doing, wherever they are,
lect on war, and peace, and
e up everything for us. The
gin in Newfoundland, and
he country like a wave as the
:00 a.m. in each time zone.
n of observing two minutes
n far from large formal cere-
ng from a heartfelt need to
to honour those who had
In fact, until the 1950s, a
ence was commonplace
st of Canada.
been several accounts of the
o minute silence, but most
gan in South Africa before
1st World War. In April, 1918,
ensive on the western front
force, and there was fear,
ed ones, but for the outcome
osses mounted, the Mayor of
arry Hands made a general
s to observe a special
14th, the noon canon
ed by a bugler playing the
"Last Post", and then "Reveille" to si
end of the silence. This was repeated
day until the Armistice was signed a
a.m. on November 11, 1918.

A local correspondent described
scene as the town fell quiet, "It was
solemn and inspiring function, the e
was magical. There was always a gre
crowd in Adderly Street at midday, b
observance seems even more strikin
less frequented streets."

A Reuters correspondent in Cape
cabled a description of the event ba
London, and from there word spread
Canada and Australia. Within a few
reports were being received in Londo
the silence was being observed in to
across the Commonwealth. At the c
sion of World War I, the two minute
became the accepted form of remem

As there are fewer and fewer sur
veterans, the Legion thinks this is a
way to pass the torch. The formal ce
monies will continue, in fact they ha
growing over the past few years and
would like to see as many Canadians
possible take part. We hope that the
Minute Wave of Silence will help the
that.

DEDICATION

AQUEDUCT, MERRITTSVILLE AND WELLAND

IS DEDICATED TO

THE PEOPLE OF THE CITY OF WELLAND,

THEIR HISTORY AND HERITAGE

TABLE OF CONTENTS

Prologue ix

PART ONE: THE BEGINNINGS

I	Origins and Explorations 3
II	The French 5
III	The British 8
IV	Struggles 9
V	The Loyalists 11
VI	Settlement 12
VII	Hardships 14
VIII	The Townships: Thorold and Crowland 17
IX	Names 22
X	Roads 23
XI	The War of 1812 25

PART TWO: THE WELLAND CANAL

XII	William Hamilton Merritt 31
XIII	Moving Forward 35
XIV	The First Welland Canal 38
XV	The Feeder 42

PART THREE: A PLACE NAMED AQUEDUCT

XVI	The First Aqueduct 49
XVII	Aqueduct: The Settlement 53
XVIII	On To Port Colborne 57

vii

PART FOUR: MERRITTSVILLE

XIX	The Second Welland Canal	63
XX	The Second Aqueduct	68
XXI	Junction Village	72
XXII	Concession 5, Lots 24 and 25	74
XXIII	Merrittsville Appears	77
XXIV	The Village	81
XXV	Industry and Commerce	84
XXVI	The Bridge on the River Welland	92
XXVII	Minds and Souls	96
XXVIII	Local Government	104

PART FIVE: THE VILLAGE OF WELLAND

| XXIX | Welland County | 111 |
| XXX | The Birth of Welland | 112 |

Epilogue	121
Appendix "A"	123
Appendix "B"	133
Appendix "C"	134
Sources	137
Illustration Credits	139
Acknowledgements	142

Prologue

On November 9, 1828, during the final days of excavation of the First Welland Canal, a portion of the canal banks collapsed near present-day Port Robinson.

The origin and development of the City of Welland can be traced directly from that construction disaster.

Part One

The Beginnings

Chapter I
Origins and Explorations

The story of the City of Welland begins with the human settlement of North America.

Most historians agree that our native people arrived from Asia more than 12,500 years ago, in a series of migrations via the Bering Strait. Looking for game, groups of hunters dispersed in all directions, and over many thousands of years, the native people fanned out through the Americas. There is evidence that the first known humans, called Early Paleo-Indians, arrived in the area of the Niagara Escarpment between 9000BC and 5000BC.

When Europeans permanently arrived in North America in the late 15th century, the principal aboriginal tribes in what is today eastern Canada were the Iroquois, Algonquins and Hurons. However, in 1649, the Iroquois invaded Huronia, destroyed the Jesuit mission that had been established near today's Midland, and almost completely wiped out the Huron confederacy. Jesuit missionaries Jean de Brébeuf and Gabriel Lalemant, since martyred, suffered horrible deaths by torture at the hands of the Iroquois.

In the Niagara Peninsula, the first inhabitants were the Neutral Indians, so named because they took no part in the wars between the Iroquois and Hurons. The Neutrals, perhaps 12,000 in number, lived in some 40 villages on a narrow strip of land along the north shore of Lake Erie, from about present-day Sarnia to Genesee, N.Y. Like the Hurons, the Neutrals came under attack from the Iroquois, were annihilated, and became extinct about 1659. Much later, the peninsula was re-settled when natives of the Chippawa nation located in the Niagara area.

Europeans first arrived in North America in the early A.D. 1000s, when Vikings from Iceland and Greenland sailed along the east coast of Canada and possibly that of the United States. Ruins of a Viking settlement have been unearthed near L'Anse aux Meadows on Newfoundland's northern peninsula, and it is believed that some Norse habitation may have remained in the area for perhaps 200 years.

A naturalized English citizen of Italian birth, John Cabot, sailing aboard the *Matthew* and financed by King Henry VII of England, touched land in June 1497, probably in Newfoundland, but permanent settlement did not follow.

CHAPTER II

THE FRENCH

The true discoverer of Canada was Jacques Cartier, who, in the spring of 1534, was commissioned by King Francis I of France to find a northwest passage to the Spice Islands (now Indonesia), in the East Indies. Leaving from the port of St. Malo in Brittany, Cartier explored the Gulf of St. Lawrence, and on July 24, 1534 planted a 30-foot cross on the Gaspé Peninsula, claiming the surrounding area for France.

Fig. 02:01   *Cartier lands on the Gaspé.*

The following year, Cartier returned to the New World, this time with three ships, and still searching for a route to the Indies, began to explore the St. Lawrence River. He wintered at Stadacona, an Indian village on the site of present-day Quebec City, and in the spring, sailed further inland. Cartier discovered another native settlement, Hochelaga, on an island in the St. Lawrence, and the name Mount Royal was given to a prominent height of land on the island.

Subsequent explorers followed, progessively expanding the territory of New

France further to the west and south. In 1608, Samuel de Champlain founded the first permanent settlement in Canada at Quebec, which he declared the capital of the colony. Champlain marked out the present site of Montreal, navigated the Ottawa River, and explored the interior as far as Georgian Bay. Later, Robert Cavelier de la Salle sailed Lake Michigan, discovered the Ohio River, and travelled to the mouth of the Mississippi River at today's New Orleans, claiming the entire river valley for France. La Salle named this vast territory Louisiana, in honour of King Louis XIV. At its height, New France comprised three-quarters of the area of North America.

La Salle visited the Niagara area in the winter of 1678-79. One of his lieutenants, Henri de Tonty, established a base camp at the mouth of the Niagara River, which later evolved into Fort Niagara in present-day Youngstown, N.Y. In December 1678, the first European permanent structure on the Niagara frontier, a storehouse, was erected at the site of Lewiston, N.Y.

The same year, Father Louis Hennepin, a Belgian missionary who came to Canada with La Salle, became the first European to visit and sketch Niagara Falls. Hennepin wrote:

> Betwixt the Lake *Ontario* and *Erié*, there is a vast and prodigious Cadence of Water which falls down after a surprizing and astonishing manner, insomuch that the Universe does not afford its parallel.

To help the French maintain control of the fur trade on the upper Great Lakes, La Salle commissioned a ship, the *Griffon*, to be built near today's Niagara Falls, N.Y. The *Griffon* sailed to the Straits of Mackinac in August 1679, but was never seen again.

An underwater wreck of a small sailing ship has been discovered in Russell Island Cove in Georgian Bay, and is considered to be the remains of the *Griffon*.

Fig. 02:02   *Hennepin at Niagara Falls.*

Chapter III
The British

Meanwhile, the British presence was established further south.

The first permanent English settlement in America began in 1607 at Jamestown, in Virginia, and shortly after, the Pilgrims arrived in Massachusetts, landing near Plymouth Rock in 1620. Sixty years later, William Penn sailed up the Delaware River and founded Pennsylvania.

By the mid 1700s, 13 vibrant, industrious and increasingly independent-thinking British colonies extended along the eastern Atlantic seaboard from New England south to Georgia.

Chapter IV

Struggles

In the early 1700s, a major conflict, the War of Spanish Succession, erupted in Europe and eventually involved many countries. The hostilities of this struggle in North America are referred to as the French and Indian Wars, and led to clashes between French and British colonists over the fur trade in the valleys of the St. Lawrence and Ohio Rivers. Along the Atlantic coast, warfare erupted between Acadia and New England.

Under the terms of the Treaty of Utrecht (1713), which concluded the war, France ceded Acadia, Newfoundland and the territories of the Hudson's Bay Company to Britain, but retained New France.

However, peace lasted for only 40 years.

Another widespread struggle, the Seven Years War, broke out in 1756, and in North America, another bitter conflict ensued between British and French forces, heavily supported by their Indian allies.

This war brought about the end of the French presence in the Niagara area, when on July 25, 1759, Fort Niagara was captured by British forces under Sir William Johnson.

Later that year, on September 13th, General James Wolfe defeated General Louis-Joseph de Montcalm at the Battle of the Plains of Abraham, probably the most significant event in Canadian history. Both Wolfe and Montcalm were killed in the battle. Montreal fell the next year and in 1760, the French governor, the Marquis de Vaudreuil-Cavagnal, surrendered New France to Great Britain.

Except for the islands of St. Pierre and Miquelon and scattered possessions in the Caribbean, thus ended the glory of France in North America.

Nevertheless, English-speaking settlement of Canada did not begin immediately, although small detachments of British soldiers with their families were posted along the frontier to scattered fortifications at Niagara, Detroit and Michilimackinac. To secure these positions, Fort Erie was built in 1764, and construction of Fort George in Niagara-on-the Lake began in 1796.

But war was to come again.

On April 19, 1775, shots were exchanged between rebels and British soldiers at Concord, in Massachusetts.

The American Revolution had begun.

Chapter V
The Loyalists

Many American colonists remained loyal to the British cause, refusing to take up arms against the Crown, and fleeing harsh repressions, left the Thirteen Colonies. Some returned to Britain, while others migrated to Canada and to the Caribbean. Eventually, between 40,000 and 60,000 of these United Empire Loyalists came to Canada. As early as 1776, Fort Niagara was receiving refugees from New York, Pennsylvania, and New Jersey, but as no settlement yet existed on the west side of the Niagara River, they remained near the fort on the east bank. The bulk of the Loyalists arrived in 1783-84.

Colonel John Butler, who had distinguished himself by leading Indian forces in the successful attack on Fort Niagara in 1759, returned to Niagara, and organized Butler's Rangers, a Loyalist troop of irregular militiamen. These forces, augmented by natives, were involved in a number of bloody massacres in upstate New York. Niagara itself was never attacked during the Revolution, and Butler's force was disbanded in June 1784. Subsequently, the Rangers were given significant land grants in the Niagara Peninsula.

After the Revolution, the Niagara River became the international boundary, and Fort Niagara was declared American property. However, the British did not immediately vacate the fort, since the United States government owed restitution to many Loyalists for property that had been taken from them during the Revolution. Finally, the British moved out in 1796, and the American flag flew over Fort Niagara.

Chapter VI

Settlement

As the number of refugees at Fort Niagara grew, the problem of finding land for them became acute. British authorities decided that settlement of these displaced persons should begin on the west side of the river, as the east bank was considered too marshy, and also more vulnerable to American attack. Accordingly, a strip of land, four miles wide, between Lake Ontario and Lake Erie, was purchased from the Mississauga Indians. By early 1782, this settlement had achieved a population of nearly 70 inhabitants, mainly located at Niagara, Chippawa and Fort Erie. Later, this number increased to over 600 with the disbandment of Butler's Rangers. In 1789, the population of the Niagara Peninsula was estimated at 3,100; ten years later, this figure was approaching 6,000.

In 1784, a further purchase from the Mississaugas (the selling price was 1180 pounds, 7 shillings and 4 pence), extended government ownership of land westward to Burlington Bay, and included all the Niagara Peninsula. Most of the Mississaugas relocated to a reserve on the banks of the Grand River, although a few remained in the peninsula.

Land grants from 50 to 1,000 acres, according to military rank, were given to disbanded soldiers, while Loyalist settlers were granted 100 acres for the head of each family, plus a further 50 acres for each additional member of the family. These grants were supplemented with some livestock, implements and a supply of provisions for one year.

In 1792, a plan was laid out for a town which was to become Newark, later named Niagara, and eventually Niagara-on-the-Lake. The Lieutenant-Governor, Colonel John Graves Simcoe, declared Newark the capital of Upper Canada, now Ontario, and the first Assembly of the Provincial Parliament was held there on September 18, 1792.

After Fort Niagara was delivered up to the Americans in 1796, Simcoe

Fig. 06:01   *Lieutenant-Governor Simcoe arrives at the first Parliament of Upper Canada.*

determined to move the capital from Newark to a safer site further from the frontier, and York, now Toronto, was chosen.

By 1807, the Canadian side of the Niagara River was described as one settled street from Lake Ontario to Lake Erie, with the villages of Chippawa and Fort Erie each containing about 20 houses.

Settlers spread out from the west bank of the Niagara River through Niagara and Stamford Townships, and then westward along the Lake Ontario shore. These lands were considered desirable locations, as they were well drained, accessible by many waterways such as the Twelve Mile Creek, and enjoyed a more moderate climate.

However, habitation of the southern Niagara Peninsula proceeded more slowly since much of the land above the Niagara Escarpment, and particularly near Lake Erie, was marshy and/or poorly drained. Nevertheless, by the late 1780s settlement of these areas was well underway. For example, a family named Buchner left their home on Staten Island, N.Y., and arrived in Crowland Township as early as 1778. A hundred families located at Sugar Loaf Point, west of Port Colborne; some of the Sugar Loaf settlers may have arrived in Canada by crossing Lake Erie on the winter ice.

Chapter VII

Hardships

The settlers did not enjoy an easy life.

Even getting to the Niagara frontier created much hardship. The journey involved a long trek by horseback, or by foot, through the forest wilderness of Pennsylvania and western New York, which in many areas were inhabited by hostile Indians. Then came the challenge of fording the wide and swift Niagara River.

Fig. 07:01   *The long journey.*

Late in the 1700s, the northern part of the Niagara Peninsula was a dense forest; pine, oak, maple and hickory grew to great heights, with thick and heavy underbrush. It is said that a settler could burn off an acre of forest in three weeks; then, with back-breaking labour, the land had to be cleared of fallen trees and stumps.

The pioneer's first cabin was built from round logs, the spaces between filled and packed with clay. Long-time residents of Welland can remember the log cabin in Chippawa Park, typical of this type of dwelling. Sometimes, such a house was built by a gathering of neighbours and completed in one day. Windows were often made from oiled paper, as glass was not readily available on the frontier.

Fig. 07:02   *Clearing the land.*

Once the land was cleared and crops planted, grown and harvested, the problem then arose of getting the grain to a mill. In the early days of settlement, only two mills were in existence in the southern peninsula, one at St. Johns, the other at Niagara Falls. Thus, this journey often involved a long and arduous trek along Indian trails through the dense forest. If the settler was fortunate to have his land located on or near the Chippawa Creek or Lyon's Creek, some of the journey could be made by canoe or raft.

At times, nature savaged the pioneers. Seventeen eighty-eight has been called "the year of the famine". Heavy frosts occured during the summer of that year, even snow in July, and much of the crops was destroyed. It is said that families made do with two or three ears of corn for days on end. Even boughs, leaves and bark were eaten. The military also suffered; troops garrisoned in the Niagara area were reduced to a ration of one biscuit a day.

Two or three good years of harvest followed the freeze. But on July 1, 1792, a violent storm swept through Pelham and Thorold Townships, cutting a swath of destruction, and considerable damage was done to crops as well as settlers' buildings and possessions. Every tree in the path of the storm was levelled.

The strip of downed timber was later cleared away, the ground levelled, and a roadway laid along the path of the destruction. To this day, that road between Fonthill and Port Robinson is called Hurricane Road.

Disaster struck again in the summer of 1819, when forest fires raged through Niagara and consumed many buildings and crops. Page's *Illustrated Historical Atlas of the Counties of Lincoln & Welland, Ont.* (1876) relates: "Owing to the drought which had continued some months everything was dry as tinder, and at night the flames sweeping everything down before them could be seen for many miles."

It was not an easy life.

Chapter VIII

The Townships: Thorold and Crowland

Of special significance to the history of the City of Welland are Thorold and Crowland Townships, as it was from a portion of these two municipalities that the Village of Welland was created in 1858. The boundary between the two townships is the Welland River; Thorold Township is west and north of the river, Crowland Township lies to the east and south.

Many of the Thorold Township lots that have become part of Welland were acquired in 1796 by Captain Thomas Welch, and also by Robert Hamilton, a prominent and prosperous Queenston merchant and land speculator. In 1799, Hamilton bought 7,900 acres of land in what is now Welland County, which, however, were registered to him as Crown grants. Welch and Hamilton also acquired extensive holdings in Crowland Township, including what is today downtown Welland.

After the Revolution, a group of Quakers settled in the southern part of Thorold Township, locating on land owned by Hamilton. Because of their religious beliefs, the Quakers had not taken an active part in the Revolution, but instead chose to remain under British authority. In time, this area became known as the Quaker Road settlement, and by 1816, had sufficient population to warrant the building of the first Quaker Road School. Some of these pioneer Quaker families, such as the Gainers and Goodwillies, remained in the area for several generations.

In those early days, Quaker Road extended further east than at present, crossing the Chippawa Creek, now the Welland River, at Misener's Bridge, which was constructed in 1821. (There was as yet no Welland Canal.) At the river, the road turned sharply southeast to Cook's Mills, and continued across Crowland Township to Zavitz's Mills in Bertie Township. A small part of this road remains today northwest of Cook's Mills, and is named Old Quaker Road. On the following map, this roadway is referred to as the Nigah Road.

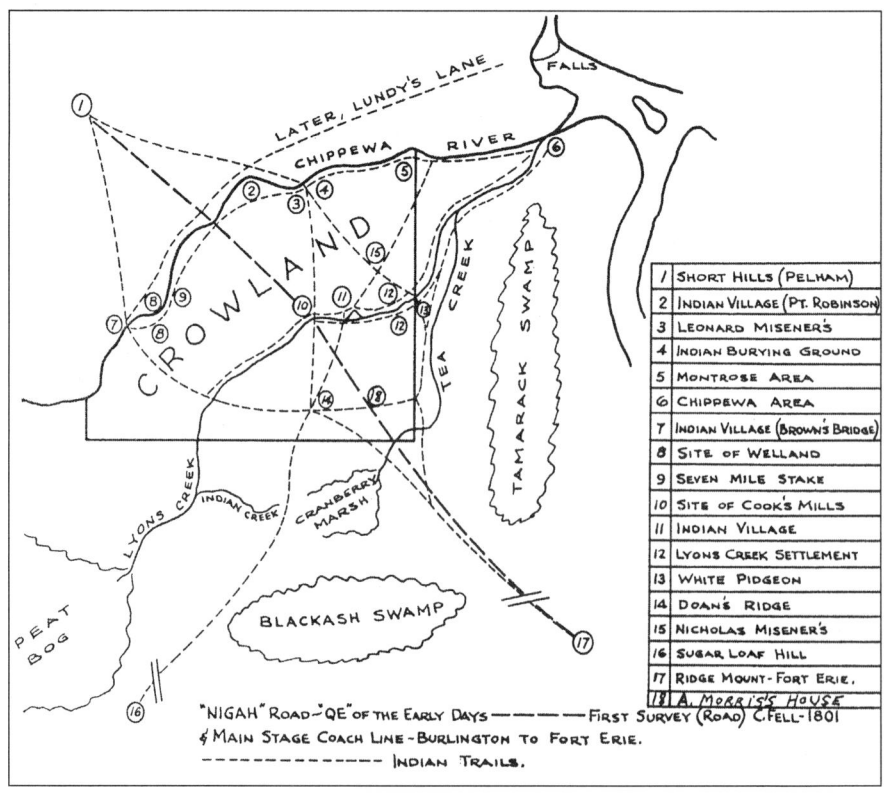

Fig. 08:01   *The Nigah Road between the Short Hills① and Bertie Township.⑰*

In 1794, a young Scot, Thomas Bald, settled in Thorold Township on a 200-acre grant north of the Chippawa Creek. The farm was originally located between today's Thorold Road and Fitch Street, and extended from Willson Road east to First Avenue. The Bald family also owned another farm near present-day West Main Street. Several streets in that area, such as Bald Street, Catherine Street and Jane Street (now Maple Avenue), were named after the Bald family and its members. The former James C. Bald School on Thorold Road was named after the grandson of Thomas Bald.

It is said that Merritt Island is Welland's best kept secret. Part of the island once was the farmland of Jonathan Silverthorne, who came to Canada in 1812, and built a log cabin on the west bank of the Chippawa Creek. His farm extended from Quaker Road south to Woodlawn Road, and from

Niagara Street east to the river. (Again, the canal wasn't there.)

In 1801, Jessie Willson purchased 262 acres in Thorold Township. His holdings were a narrow strip of land on the east side of today's Willson Road from the river north to Woodlawn Road. Glendale School and Wesley United Church are located on Willson land. The purchase price in 1801 was 131 pounds, five shillings. The current value is considerably more.

In Crowland Township, the Yokom family came north from Pennsylvania in 1799 and established a farm and grist mill on Lyon's Creek. Just prior to the War of 1812, Calvin Cook, from England, purchased Yokom's mill, then added a tannery, a sawmill and a distillery. The settlement became known as Cook's Mills, although on some early maps it is referred to as Crowland village.

In 1803, the population of Crowland was 216 persons, and in March of that year, a meeting was held to organize and name the township. Six years later, the residents numbered 554, but by 1825 the population had only increased to 637, reflecting the slow rate of growth in the area.

One of the more fascinating stories of early settlers in the Welland area is that of David Price, who was born in New York State about 1750. At the age of 21, young David and a friend, while gathering hickory nuts, were set upon and captured by a band of Seneca Indians. The companion, although wounded in the attack, was released for ransom paid by the British government, but such payment for Price was refused, and he was kept by the natives as a captive. David lived as an Indian for some seven years, and eventually was adopted as a son by Little Beard, the chief of the Seneca band.

After receiving assurances of continued affection and gratitude from the Indians, Price left the tribe at the British military installation at Oswego, N.Y. where he then served as an interpreter and clerk. After this post was evacuated at the conclusion of the American Revolution, David made his way with extreme difficulty to Fort George at Newark.

In 1816, David Price purchased from John Gray of Montreal, a 100-acre parcel of land in what is today west-side Welland, between the Welland River and Lincoln Street. Price erected a log cabin on the south bank of the river, which was later replaced by a brick home. This building eventually became the Anglican rectory and is now the site of the Niagara Regional Youth Home on Prince Charles Drive. Price was one of the very few settlers to locate in this area before the construction of the Welland Canal. In fact, at that time, only some 15 families were settled along the river in the five miles between South Pelham Street and Quaker Road.

Ellis P. Morningstar, a well-known and colourful local political personality, was a descendant of David Price.

Mention should also be made of John Brown and Brown's Bridge. John Brown was born in County Down, Ireland about 1739. As a young man, he enlisted in the 60th Royal American Regiment of Foot, a British regiment that was sent to North America, first to New York, and then to Halifax. Brown fought under Wolfe at the Battle of the Plains of Abraham. (Legend says that Wolfe died in Brown's arms.) Brown returned to Ireland where he married, and about 1774, emigrated to Pennsylvania. During the Revolution, Brown remained loyal to the Crown, and was obliged to seek refuge in Canada. He was granted 350 acres of land on the north side of the Welland River at the foot of today's South Pelham Street. The family, however, had the misfortune to arrive in the area at the time of the famine of 1788-89 and often had to sustain themselves by eating grass, roots and buds of trees.

A bridge was built across the Welland River at South Pelham Street and a small settlement that became known as Brown's Bridge was established in the vicinity. The bridge fell into disrepair, and the removal of the structure was authorized in 1868. However, some ancient timbers from the remains of Brown's bridge still protrude from the water at the foot of South Pelham Street. (Misener's bridge at Quaker Road also was abandoned in the 19th century.)

But there is more to the story of the settlement at Brown's Bridge. Population in the area was still very limited, and there was little opportunity for cultural improvement. Neverthless, a meeting was held in a nearby schoolhouse on November 26, 1825 to provide for the collection of some literature which was to be the nucleus of a circulating library.

From that meeting has directly evolved today's Welland Public Library.

Chapter IX

Names

Many place names in the Niagara Peninsula originated in Lincolnshire in England, and were chosen by Colonel John Graves Simcoe, the first Lieutenant-Governor of Upper Canada. This British county is located on the coast of the North Sea, about 100 miles north of London.

Our Welland River was named after the River Welland in Lincolnshire. The English waterway flows through very flat marshland, is navigable for some 25 miles, and enters the North Sea at the Wash. The original designation of the river in Niagara was the Chippawa Creek, but was officially changed to the present name by a proclamation issued by Lt.-Gov. Simcoe in 1792. The canal, as originally conceived, was a canal from the Welland River, and thus was named the Welland Canal.

Crowland is an ancient Lincolnshire town on the River Welland. Saxon King Ethelbert founded a monastery at Crowland, sometimes spelled Croyland, in the year 716. This abbey was later destroyed by the Danes in 871. Crowland is noted for the unique medieval triangular Trinity Bridge, built in the 13th century, although some sources date the bridge to 941.

Stamford is another old Lincolnshire town, whose name is derived from a stone ford across the River Welland at that point. Wainfleet is named for a marsh in Lincolnshire; other Niagara Peninsula names that originated in this area of England are Humberstone, Grimsby and Saltfleet.

The name Niagara is, of course, of Indian origin.

Chapter X

Roads

The roads of the early settlers largely followed the course of native trails. The longest and most important in the Niagara Peninsula was the Iroquois Trail, which in turn was part of the major east-west aboriginal route in eastern North America, extending from Detroit (and perhaps St. Louis) to Albany, N.Y. In Niagara, the old Highway 8 (now Regional Road 81), and St. Paul Street in downtown St. Catharines, are part of the Iroquois Trail.

Many aboriginal trails closely followed the course of rivers and creeks. In some instances, a river had two trails, one on each side of the waterway. Such was the case with the Chippawa Creek. The trail on the north and west side of the river between Chippawa and Port Robinson is today's Chippawa Creek Road, which continues to become the roadway on Merritt Island, and then Colbeck Drive. This was all one continuous trail, before the construction of the canal.

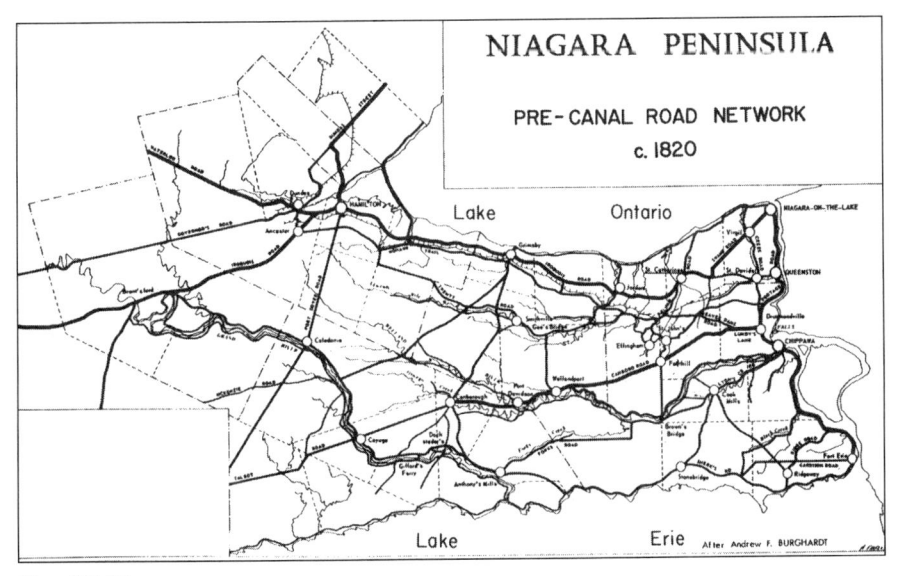

Fig. 10:01

In present-day Welland, the trail from Chippawa on the south and east bank of the Welland River is today's River Road and East Main Street, but before the 1840s, was named, appropriately, the Chippawa Road. This road becomes the present West Main Street and Riverside Drive, and continues on to Wellandport and beyond.

(In the early days of Thorold Township, Colbeck Drive was also called the Chippawa Road.)

Soon after settlement, Thorold and Crowland Townships were surveyed, and the resulting grid pattern of concession line roads was overlaid upon the Indian routes. Some of these original trails and roads were retained, but many were not, and almost all traces of most of them have disappeared.

Chapter XI
The War of 1812

Within 30 years of the arrival of the first settlers, war came again to the Niagara Peninsula.

It is not the purpose of this work to detail the causes and history of the War of 1812. However, the Niagara area was heavily involved in the struggle. Queenston Heights, Lundy's Lane, Cook's Mills, Beaverdams, Fort Erie and Stoney Creek all saw military action. Names such as Sir Isaac Brock and Laura Secord are, or should be, as familiar to Canadians as Stonewall Jackson and Davy Crockett.

Niagara suffered grievously in the war, with much of the peninsula overrun by the invading forces. Farmhouses and barns, villages and towns were burnt and destroyed. Livestock, grain and food were carried off, and many dwellings were plundered of possessions. Queenston and St. David's suffered heavy damage, and the town of Niagara was destroyed by fire. The enemy took many civilian prisoners, who were deported under guard to the United States.

The final skirmish of the war, the Battle of Cook's Mills, was fought on October 29, 1814 within the present-day boundaries of the City of Welland. An American detachment of 1,000 men was positioned with their guns pointing east, as this was the direction from which a British attack was expected. A scout conveyed this information to the Glengarry Light Infantry, advancing from Chippawa, who then altered their route of advance, and with a force of 500 men, attacked the American position from the rear. This surprise tactic completely disorganized the invaders, and they fled in panic back to the United States. The British and Canadian losses numbered 19, while the Americans suffered 67 casualties.

The cairn and plaque in Cook's Mills that today commemorates this skirmish, is depicted below.

Fig. 11:01   *The cairn on the site of the Battle of Cook's Mills.*

In 1814, the Treaty of Ghent ended the war, but the effects of the conflict were felt in the Niagara Peninsula for many years.

It may be of interest to relate a final, but not well known, story about the war.

In 1812, the question was raised with General Isaac Brock as to the possible defensive significance of the height of land in the Short Hills in Pelham Township, but Brock replied that he did not have sufficient forces at the time to man such a position.

A decade after the war, the British government proposed the construction of a dozen fortifications in Canada, one of which was to be a major installation in the Short Hills. This plan required that almost 900 acres of land that comprised the highest part of this terrain be purchased, along with adjacent areas.

The chosen site was surveyed, mapped and named "Wellington Height", after the Duke of Wellington. One strong point of the proposed fortress was to be called "King George's Battery". It was remembered that during the recent war, the peninsula had been occupied by the invaders, and it was considered that if the Americans were to come again, such a military installation would provide a protective overview of a large area, as well as a formidable defensive position.

The great scheme got as far as buying some of the required land, and there it stopped.... forever. The Duke of Wellington had become British prime minister, and a time of governmental fiscal austerity was developing. The plan for the fortress was repeatedly deferred, and then in the 1860s, finally abandoned. The land for "Wellington Height" was sold off as farmland.

However, had this immense fortification been constructed, it would have been located in Fonthill on the site of the parking lot, clubhouse and first tee of Lookout Point Golf and Country Club.

(Lookout Point was founded by a group of Welland sportsmen in 1922, and thus today is the city's oldest golf course.)

Before the War of 1812, progress in the Niagara Peninsula had been slow but steady, but this advance was halted by the conflict. After hostilities ceased, the settlers struggled to regain their previous well-being, but the damage suffered in the war made recovery difficult and slow.

Organized settlements and the centres of economic activity remained near the periphery of the peninula. Along the Niagara River, Niagara, Queenston and Chippawa were significant centres, while below the escarpment, such settlements as St.Catharines, Jordan and Grimbsy, situated where creeks and streams intersected the Iroquois Trail, were developing. However, with the exception of St. Johns, most of the interior of the peninsula was devoid of organized communities.

This situation was to change profoundly with the coming of the Welland Canal.

Part Two

The Welland Canal

Chapter XII

William Hamilton Merritt

William Hamilton Merritt is undoubtedly the predominant figure in the history of the Niagara Peninsula.

Merritt was born in Bedford, Westchester County, N.Y. on July 3, 1793. His father, Thomas, had fought as a Loyalist in the Colonies during the American Revolution, and after the war, resided in New Brunswick for a short time, then returned briefly to the United States. The family came to Canada again in 1796, and settled in the Niagara Peninsula on the Twelve Mile Creek, where a number of the Merritts' neighbours were former members of Butler's Rangers.

William Hamilton Merritt attended school in Burlington, studying mathematics and field surveying.

As a young man, Merritt became a partner in a store at Shipman's Corners, now St. Catharines. It is interesting to note that in those early days, much trade was transacted by barter, since currency was then in short supply. Just before the onset of the War of 1812, he sold his interest in the store, and returned to the family 200-acre farm on the Twelve Mile Creek.

With war underway, Merritt joined the Second Lincoln Militia, stationed at Chippawa. He recounted in later years that constant patrols along the Niagara River first suggested to him the idea of a possible canal through the peninsula. Later in the war, after seeing military action at Queenston and Stoney Creek, Merritt stumbled into American lines at the battle of Lundy's Lane and was captured by the enemy. He was held as a prisoner of war in Massachusetts until his release in March 1815.

When hostilities ceased, Merritt purchased 25 acres at Shipman's Corners, and built a large house, part for a dwelling and part for a store. He also sold goods further afield at Niagara and Queenston. Carrying on business at that time was complicated by many difficulties, one of which was poor communications. In a letter, he complained about Canadian postal service being expensive and conveyance slow.

In 1816, Merritt acquired a rundown sawmill on the Twelve Mile Creek, which he soon had up and running, and then built a grist mill and erected a store. A salt spring was located on his property on the creek, and there he began to manufacture salt at a time when that commodity was very expesive, selling at $10 to $15 a barrel. Later, he became involved in the production of potash. Merritt was an aggressive and ambitious promoter and entreprneur.

Fig. 12:01   *William Hamilton Merritt.*

The uncertainty of a sufficient supply of water in the dry, warmer weather was always a problem for the mills on the Twelve Mile Creek; in the summer of 1818, the scarcity of water became particularly acute. Perhaps remembering his thoughts from years earlier about a canal, Merritt conceived the idea of bringing a supply of water to his mills from the Welland River.

However, Merritt was not the first to put forward the idea of a canal crossing the Niagara Peninsula. In 1799, Robert Hamilton, the Queenston merchant mentioned previously, headed a group that unsucccessfully petitioned the Upper Canada Legislature for the construction of a canal between Fort Erie and Queenston. Later, in 1817 and 1818, a number of other proposed routes for a canal were put forward. At that time, goods being shipped to the upper Great Lakes were transported by boat to Queenston, unloaded onto wagons and hauled upstream and around Niagara Falls for five hours and eleven miles along the Portage Road to Chippawa. Here the cargo was loaded back onto boats. This was an expensive and time-consuming procedure, and thus the idea of a canal was received with favour in many quarters.

Another significant factor was the Erie Canal, which was soon to be completed between the Hudson River and Lake Erie through upstate New York. It was obvious that goods from the upper lakes would soon be sent to Buffalo and on to New York City, thus bypassing Montreal. But it was a lack of water that moved the concept forward, and resulted ultimately in the development of a canal.

Accordingly, Merritt borrowed a surveying instrument called a water level from Samuel Beckett, a mill owner in St. Johns, and with George Keefer, John DeCew and other neighbours, set out to explore a posssible route for a waterway. They started at the headwaters of a branch of the Twelve Mile Creek near present-day Allanburg, and ran a line two miles south to the Welland River.

A ridge of land was encountered between their starting point and the river, and was calculated as rising to a height of 30 feet. However, whether due to a faulty instrument or to the lack of skill in using the water level, their measurement was incorrect; the ridge was actually 60 feet high.

This miscalculation led directly to events that developed into what today is the City of Welland.

Chapter XIII

Moving Forward

On July 4, 1818, shortly after the surveying expedition, Merritt organized a meeting in St. Catharines, from which a petition was sent to the Provincial Legislature requesting an act to provide for the construction of the proposed canal to connect the Twelve Mile Creek and the Welland River. However, by this time the concept had been expanded to that of a waterway to carry boats, not just to supply water. The amount of £2,000 was approved for a survey of the Welland route, as well as for possible canals on the St. Lawrence River.

However, the route surveyed in the Niagara Peninsula began at the Grand River and terminated at Burlington Bay, a distance of 50 miles, but this scheme, of course, provided no water to the mills on the Twelve Mile Creek. Obviously, nothing came of this proposal.

In 1823, funds were solicited to employ an engineer, Hiram Tibbetts, to make a new survey for the canal route. Tibbetts recommended that a channel beginning at present-day Port Robinson be dug at a level four feet below the surface of the Welland River, proceed north from the river to the headwaters of a branch of the Twelve Mile Creek at today's Allanburg, and thence northwest to DeCew's Falls (and, of course, DeCew's mill).

Here Tibbetts suggested that the escarpment be descended by an incline marine railway (such as seen today at Big Chute on the Trent-Severn Waterway) and that the canal then follow the Twelve Mile Creek to Lake Ontario at Port Dalhousie.

On January 19, 1824 an act of the Upper Canada Legislature provided for the formation of the Welland Canal Company, with capitalization of $150,000, divided into shares of $50 each.

(It should be noted that in the early 19th century, both dollars and pounds were in common usage in Upper Canada, and monetary values have been quoted in this work as they appear in the original sources.)

Merritt was the financial agent for the company; to raise capital for the venture, he travelled extensively to York, Kingston, Montreal and Quebec, as well as to the United States and Great Britain.

Later in 1824, a revised route was put forward for the Welland Canal. This version followed Tibbett's line from Port Robinson to Allanburg, but then continued north to Marlatt's Pond in Thorold, and descended the escarpment by locks near present Bradley Street and Glendale Avenue in Merritton. The route continued via Dick's Creek through the valley behind today's St. Catharines General Hospital, and then followed part of the route of what is now Highway 406 in the city's downtown. The canal then joined the Twelve Mile Creek, and continued to the lake at Port Dalhousie. This route required the construction of 40 wooden locks, the majority of which were to ascend the escarpment in present-day Thorold and Merritton.

Tibbett's east branch line as proposed in 1823, and the eventual route of the canal, are depicted in Fig. 13.01.

The company's stock was now totally subscribed except for $30,000. Accordingly, the directors felt that they could proceed with the canal construction, and tenders were put out.

On St. Andrew's Day, November 30, 1824, about 200 persons gathered at the head of one of the branches of the Twelve Mile Creek near today's Allanburg to witness the historic ceremony of turning the first sod for the Welland Canal.

It is appropriate to quote part of Merritt's address that day:

> We are assembled here this day for the purpose of removing the first earth from a canal which will, with the least, and by the shortest distance, connect the greatest extent of inland waters, in the

whole world.... We were fully aware of the supposed magnitude of the undertaking; we.... determined to.... apply.... our own shoulders to the wheel, and set about it in good earnest.

This event, so important to the history of the City of Welland, is commemmorated today by a cairn at the west approach to the Allanburg bridge.

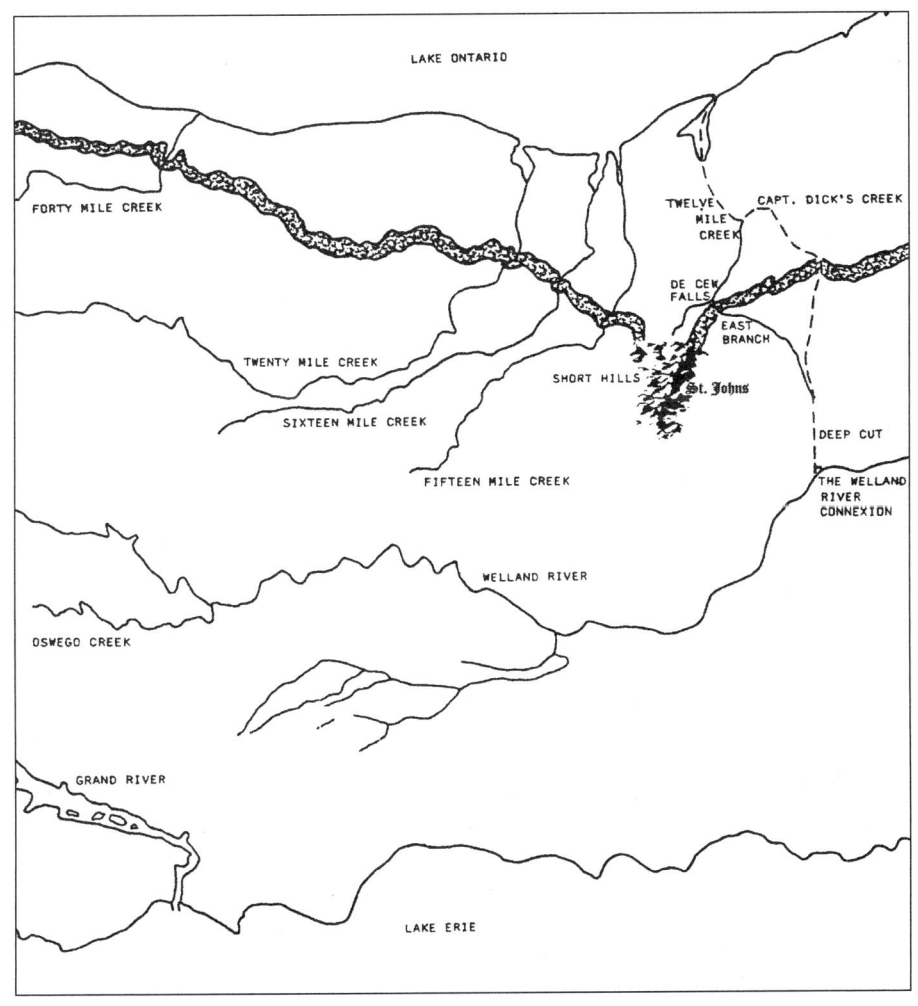

Fig. 13:01 *Proposed and final routes of the First Welland Canal.*

CHAPTER XIV

THE FIRST WELLAND CANAL

In November 1824, about 40 tenders for the canal construction were put out, and in January 1825, contracts were let for the work between the Welland River and Lake Ontario, including 40 wooden locks of white pine, at a tendered price of £550 each. Construction began in July 1825, using, where possible, natural waterways such as the Twelve Mile Creek, Dick's Creek, Marlatt's Pond and the Welland River.

IMPORTANT TO
LABOURERS.
THE encouragement given at the
DEEP CUT
is such, that the Common Labourer is actually receiving from
Thirteen to Seventeen
DOLLARS per month, besides a number of PREMIUMS to be distributed when the work is completed, among those averaging the most labour. It continues very healthy here—only one having died, out of 800 labourers and about 150 families, for the last two weeks.
OLIVER PHELPS.
Deep Cut, Sept. 5, 1827.　　a5

Fig. 14:01

Undoubtedly, the most challenging part of the entire project was the excavation through the height of land between Port Robinson and Allanburg, that came to be called the "Deep Cut." This involved digging a cut over two miles in length, at times to a depth of 70 feet, from which over one million cubic yards of earth were removed. The construction was very labour-intensive. Some 250 men (some sources say 600) were employed at one time, at a daily wage rate of 63 cents.

The work was heavy and difficult, accomplished by human brawn and helped only by crude tools and animals. The earth was loosened by pick and shovel, moved from the site by wheelbarrow, then loaded onto ox-drawn carts or wagons pulled by horses. If the banks were very steep, mud was sometimes shovelled into sacks, and carried to the surface upon men's backs. To expedite the excavation, a competition with a prize of $500 was held to come up with a machine to remove the greatest quantity of earth in a given time for the least expense. The winning design was submitted by Oliver Phelps, a contractor on the canal, and involved a wheel, ropes and hooks by which oxen and carts in tandem moved in and out of the excavation. The progress of moving earth was greatly accelerated by this novel innovation.

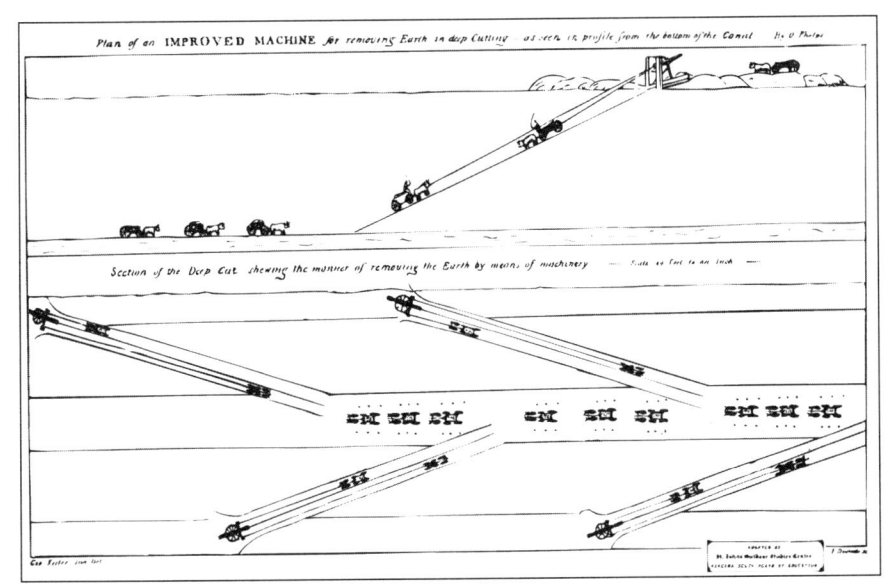

Fig. 14:02   *Phelps' earth-moving machine.*

The work was not without danger. Unstable soil conditions were encountered in many places. Rock had to be drilled by hand and then blown apart with gunpowder. It was once boasted that there had only been three deaths "in a considerable period of time."

Disease also took a toll. Due to the conditions of moving immense quantities of wet earth, many labourers developed a malaria-like sickness, and fell ill with fever; cholera likewise was a grave problem. Even the work animals suffered. Numerous oxen were killed by sliding down the deep banks that became slippery after rains, and many horses died from injury and infection.

The expression "grog-man" is frequently found in pay lists of the canal company. This may help to account for the unprecedented amount of work that was accomplished each day.

In 1825, the Erie Canal through New York State between Albany and Buffalo was completed, and experienced engineers, contractors and labourers from that work were available for the Welland project.

Immigrants too joined the work force. Many came from Ireland, and unfortunately, difficulties arose from religious and political differences that were brought from their homeland. It was not uncommon for violence to break out.

Many of these workers came with their families, and settled in shanties that were often dismantled and moved to other construction sites as the work progressed. It has already been mentioned that communities had earlier been established primarily around the periphery of the peninsula. Now, along the canal route, new settlements were beginning to spring up, which in time developed into Port Dalhousie, Merritton, Thorold, Allanburg and Port Robinson.

Later events gave rise to Welland, Dain City, Humberstone, Port Colborne, Marshville (now Wainfleet), Stromness and Dunnville. Commercial and industrial activity began to shift to the interior of the peninsula, and communities not on the canal line, such as Niagara, Queenston and Chippawa slowly began to decline. The progress of St. Catharines, which had been established before the canal, was accelerated by the new waterway, and that community became the pre-eminent centre of the peninsula.

The economic structure of the Niagara Peninsula was being changed forever by the Welland Canal.

In the meantime, work on the canal was proceeding at an entirely different location. In 1825, plans were finalized that, in effect, created two canal channels between Port Robinson and Lake Erie, with two entrances to the lake. The original route of the canal that crossed the peninsula between Lake Ontario and the Welland River, remained unchanged. However, at Port Robinson, the two routes diverged. The eastern branch would proceed via the Welland River to Chippawa and the Niagara River, and against heavy current, continue upstream to Buffalo and Lake Erie. The western branch was to follow the Welland River from Port Robinson to the Forks Creek, some four miles west of present-day Welland, and then connect with the Grand

River and Lake Erie by a 12-mile channel cut through the Wainfleet Marsh.

As the work on the Deep Cut was stopped in September 1827 due to heavy rains, and was not resumed until the following April, excavation in the Wainfleet area was pushed vigourously in the fall of 1827 and the spring of 1828. The millrace that exists today in Wainfleet is part of that construction, and thus is one of the very few remaining traces of the First Welland Canal.

Then disaster struck!

Heavy rains continued through 1828, and the high banks of the Deep Cut, already supporting the great weight of the excavated earth, were softened.

On November 9, 1828, with only two weeks of work remaining to complete the undertaking, the banks at the south end of the Deep Cut near Port Robinson gave way, and collapsed into the excavated canal channel, causing some loss of life. Further landslides soon followed.

In attempting to dig down through the fallen earth, extensive loose sand was encountered and it quickly became evident that it would not be possible to make an excavation deep enough for the Welland River to provide a source of water for the Welland Canal.

This calamity led to the digging of the Feeder Canal and the construction of an aqueduct over the Welland River.

A settlement became established at the construction site of the aqueduct, and in due course, the ensuing shantytown evolved into what is today the City of Welland.

Chapter XV

The Feeder

Now the challenge arose of finding an alternate and higher source of water for the canal.

As noted earlier, excavation had begun near present-day Wainfleet village to connect the Welland and Grand Rivers. In December 1828, it was proposed that a dam be constructed near the mouth of the Grand to elevate that river to the height necessary to overcome the slippage at the Deep Cut. From this dam, a channel could be dug to feed this higher water level across the Wainfleet Marsh to the Welland River, which would be crossed by an aqueduct, and the Feeder then continue on to Port Robinson.

Construction of the dam soon began at the proposed location on the Grand River. However, naval authorities, still mindful of the War of 1812, and concerned that at this site the structure could be vulnerable to possible enemy action, halted the work. An alternative placement, five miles upstream was recommended, and the dam was then completed at this new location, which became the site of present-day Dunnville.

In April 1829, as soon as the frost was out of the ground, work began on the Feeder itself. The contractor advised that 1,000 labourers were required, and many were transferred from the Deep Cut to the new project. The entire job was completed in 177 days, a remarkable achievement for those days, and water was able to be let into both the Feeder and the main canal in November 1829. Although the canal from Lake Ontario to Port Robinson was opened to navigation later that month, the first transit of the Feeder did not occur until the following spring, when two barges were transported to Dunnville on May 10, 1830.

The Feeder Canal began immediately above the dam in today's downtown Dunnville, and followed a route to Stromness, where it began a straight line across the Wainfleet Marsh, to near the west end of the present Broadway

Street bridge in Welland South. There the channel turned north, roughly along the west bank of the disused Fourth Welland Canal (now the recreational waterway) in downtown Welland, and crossed over the Welland River through a wooden aqueduct located just east of today's Niagara Street bridge. From the aqueduct, the Feeder followed the present-day bend of the river and continued north to Port Robinson, where, through two locks, it emptied into the Welland River.

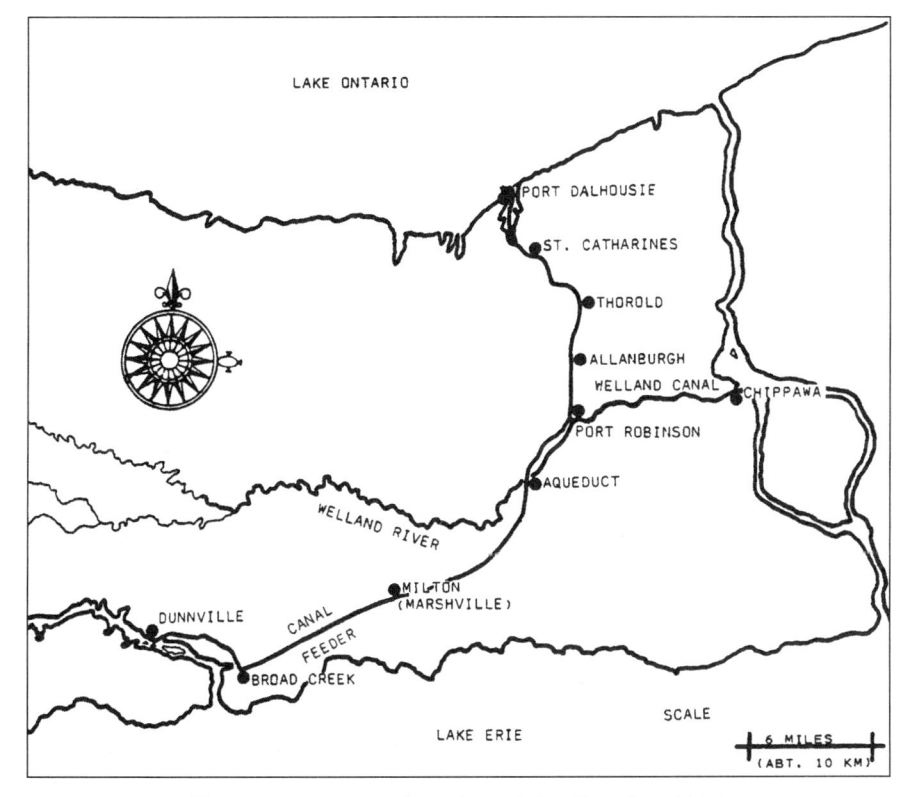

Fig. 15:01   *The First Welland Canal, and the Feeder, 1829.*

Part of the Feeder was excavated through the farm of David Price, albeit with much opposition from Price, who went so far as to tear out the survey stakes for the canal route through his property. Nevertheless, in spite of these differences, Price managed to remain on good terms with William Hamilton Merritt.

Although the original route of the Feeder was from Dunnville to Port Robinson, the section between Welland South and Port Robinson became the line of the First Welland Canal, and only that portion from Dunnville to Welland South retained the name, the Feeder Canal. But even that title became a misnomer, as the waterway also carried vessels, and thus served as more than just a channel to feed water to the Welland Canal.

Today, much of this Feeder Canal is still evident between Stromness and Welland South. It may be readily seen from Humberstone Road, immediately before the entrance to the Welland landfill site, and following Feeder Road, from Forks Road to Wainfleet village, Stromness and beyond. Also, a section of the original Welland Canal Feeder still exists between Port Robinson and Quaker Road, as an overgrown ditch on the west side of Towpath Road; a continuation of this section can be observed as a depression behind the rear parking lot of Seaway Mall in Welland.

Fig. 15:02   *The First Welland Canal as seen today, beside Towpath Road.*

On St. Andrew's Day, November 30, 1829, five years to the day after the first shovelful of earth was removed at Allanburg, the first transit of the

Welland Canal was accomplised by two schooners, one Canadian, the other American.

The *Annie and Jane* from York (Toronto) and the R.H. Broughton from Youngstown, N.Y., both especially hired for the occasion, and gaily festooned with flags, emblems and pennants, and with William Hamilton Merritt on board, left Port Dalhousie, to the cheers of a large crowd. Two days later, both arrived under sail, at Buffalo. On December 3rd, the *Annie and Jane* returned through the canal to Lake Ontario.

Fig. 15:03   *The opening of the First Welland Canal, November 30, 1829.*

William Hamilton Merritt's mighty undertaking was now complete, and at long last, navigation between Lake Ontario and Lake Erie became a reality.

WELLAND CANAL.

PUBLICK NOTICE is hereby given, that the WELLAND CANAL is now open for the passage of Vessels, from Lake Erie to Lake Ontario.

By order of the Board of Directors,
JAMES BLACK, *Sec'y.*

*Welland Canal Office,
St. Catharines. Nov.* 30, 1829.

Part Three

A Place Named Aqueduct

CHAPTER XVI

THE FIRST AQUEDUCT

The most significant construction project of the first canal relevant to the present-day City of Welland, was the wooden aqueduct that carried the waters of the canal over the Welland River.

As related above, it was apparent after the collapse of the banks at the Deep Cut in November 1828, that the Welland River could not be used as a water source for the canal. Subsequently, James Geddes, an American canal engineer, recommended to the directors of the canal company that a feeder be dug from the Grand River, that the water from this source be carried across the Welland River by means of an aqueduct, and that the feeder then continue on to Port Robinson.

The following January, a proposal was accepted that this aqueduct be constructed near Helm's (sometimes spelled Hellem's) Creek. (This stream, which arose near the present Broadway Street and flowed north to empty into the river just east of today's Niagara Street bridge, has long since disappeared, probably at the time of the excavation of the Third Welland Canal in the 1880s.) Later that month, a bid of £875 from Oliver Phelps, T. Brundage and Marshall Lewis was accepted for the construction of the aqueduct, and the work commenced late in February 1829.

A brief reference to the building of the aqueduct is found in a letter of March 24, 1829 from Merritt's wife, Catharine, to her parents in Mayville, N.Y., in which she recounts an overnight sleighing expedition from St. Catharines to Dunnville and return. Mrs. Merritt wrote that the group passed by the supporting piers that had been sunk for the new aqueduct.

Much of the required timber for the structure came from sources along the Welland River, and these logs were floated down to the construction area. In May, the company directors visited the work site and noted that all the timber and other construction material had been delivered, the four piers were sunk, and the main frame was up. By August, the aqueduct was complete.

It was later reported that the total paid for the structure was £1,525.

It is unfortunate that no original plans or diagrams of this first aqueduct have survived. Of course, the construction in 1829 preceded photography, and thus no pictures as such are in existence. The location, however, is precisely known, and we are aware of the dimensions of the structure. But what this aqueduct actually looked like will probably never be known, although a sketch by Fonthill artist Fran Peacock of the possible appearance of the wooden aqueduct is reproduced below.

Fig. 16:01   *The First Welland Canal aqueduct, as rendered by artist Fran Peacock.*

The west bank of the original canal ran very close to the West Main Street end of the still-standing lift bridge, and in width extended to about the concrete pier supporting the bridge's west tower. From that point, the canal went north to the river and the aqueduct.

(It should be noted that until the construction in the 1920s of the Fourth Welland Canal, now the recreational waterway, the river flowed directly east from the Niagara Street bridge, then under the former swimming pool, which was the aqueduct for the second canal, through the area of the wading pool, and turned north near Dorothy Street. The hill leading down to the lower-level parking area behind the Court House, is the original riverbank.)

South of today's Lincoln Street, a water-filled ravine adjoined the west side of the canal. The marshy wet land that was visible until recently at the foot of Denistoun Street, was a remanent of that ravine.

The aqueduct, constructed of white pine, was located about 165 feet east of the present Niagara Street bridge, approximately at the end of today's Seeley

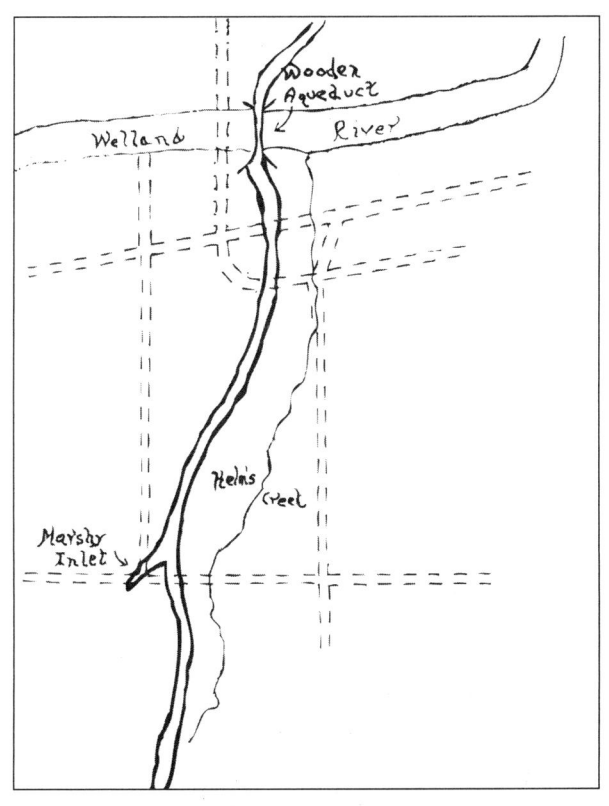

Fig. 16:02   *The route of the first canal through present-day Welland. Current streets are indicated by dotted lines.*

Street. The structure, which was 365 feet long and 24 feet wide, carried a towpath on the east side, and was supported by four piers, each 15 by 40 feet. The aqueduct was sufficiently high above the surface of the river to permit easy passage of boats and rafts underneath. In 1832, waste gates and valves were added that increased the length to about 600 feet.

However, the structure's wooden construction created many maintenance problems, particularly with leakage. In 1836, much of the timber work had to be repaired, and to secure the extremities, solid stone abutments were added. On August 11, 1840 a 40-foot break occurred in the aqueduct, but the damage was able to be repaired in four days. The next year, the side carrying the towpath had to be replaced.

After the stone aqueduct for the Second Welland Canal was finally completed in 1850, and no navigational need remained for the wooden aqueduct, dams were erected across the ends of the old structure. Later, the central section of the aqueduct was dismantled, and the approaches were converted into storehouses, as shown in Fig. 16:03. This plan also provides some detail of the piers and overall dimensions of the first aqueduct.

All trace of this structure has long ago disappeared, so unique and important to local history, inasmuch as the construction and maintenance of the first aqueduct was the reason for which the City of Welland of today came into being.

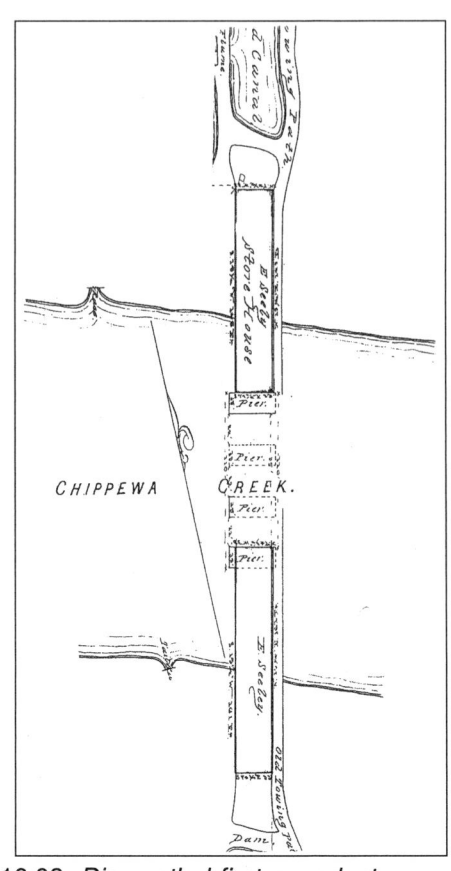

Fig. 16:03 *Dismantled first aqueduct.*

Chapter XVII

Aqueduct: The Settlement

As mentioned, the building of the first aqueduct began in February 1829, and almost immediately a settlement sprang up at the construction site. This shantytown soon became known as The Aqueduct, or more simply, Aqueduct.

If little is known about the structure called the aqueduct, even less is known about the community called Aqueduct.

Aqueduct was the forerunner of the west side of the present city, and preceded by a dozen years the appearance of any community on today's east side. Thus, Welland's west side can justifiably claim to be the oldest part of the city.

The community called Aqueduct was located near the present Niagara Street bridge, and behind the buildings that today are on the east side of the Niagara Street hill. Horses and mules were used to pull vessels through the first canal, and these animals were led and cared for by towboys. It has been suggested that stables were provided for the animals at Aqueduct and other locations along the canal, and that the towboys (the term referred to both men and boys) stayed in hotels and boarding houses along the route. Furthermore, such providers as ship chandlers, repairmen and grocers offered services and goods to vessels and their crews using the waterway. And, of course, the wooden aqueduct would have required on-going maintenance, and probably major work during the off-season when the canal was closed to navigation for the winter.

Such activities provided a large clientele for the numerous drinking establishments that quickly came into being along the line of the canal, one of which, Quinn's tavern, was located at Aqueduct. The fact that, in those days, liquor sold for 20 cents a gallon may account for the popularity of this commodity. (It has been reported that in the mid-1840s, there were 32 inns along the canal, and a further 124 bootleggers.) Near his tavern, Quinn also maintained a barn where some of the canal draught animals may have been kept. A second tavern, operated by Thomas Harper, was located between the bridge and the aqueduct.

But where did the inhabitants of Aqueduct live? Where did they work? Where did they shop? No one knows for certain.

It can be assumed that Aqueduct boasted no canal-related milling industry, although the difference in water levels between the river and the canal would have been a natural location for the establishment of mills. Indeed, the Welland Canal Company, from its inception, sold water rights for this type of industry at various locations along the line of the canal. However, little evidence exists that such development occurred at Aqueduct. In 1830, the company advertised that they were prepared to give up control of land adjacent to the canal that was not required for the actual operation of the waterway. The advertisement described various locations along the canal that included mills, but the reference to what was available at Aqueduct mentions only five acres of land, but nothing about a mill.

Furthermore, an 1847 list of mills operating along the canal makes no reference to Aqueduct. It may be noted, however, that at this time, Dunnville boasted ten mills, Allanburg four mills, Marshville (Wainfleet) sustained both a grist mill and a sawmill, and even Port Robinson had one mill. But not Aqueduct. Such industry had to await the coming of the Second Welland Canal.

Nevertheless, an 1837 map of the canal does show a sawmill located in the area of today's Rose City Seniors Centre on Lincoln Street. The mill was apparently situated on Helm's Creek and obtained its water power through a millrace from the canal, taking advantage of the difference in levels between the canal and the creek. But this mill was located too far up the canal to be considered as part of Aqueduct. The following figure depicts the location of this mill as shown on the 1837 map.

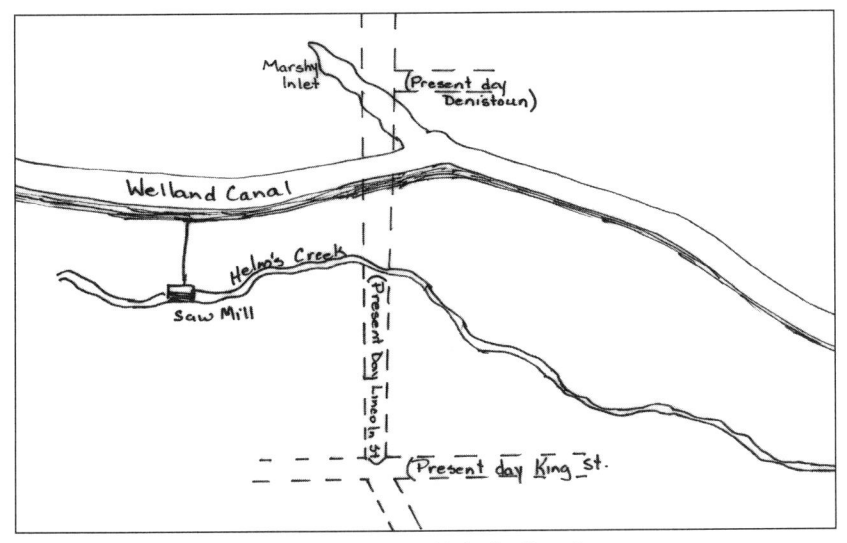

Fig. 17:01   The sawmill on Helm's Creek.

The Chippawa Road, now East Main Street, crossed the first canal at Aqueduct by means of a wooden swing bridge. This bridge, which was turned by pushing heavy paddles or beams, is depicted below. Also, it is likely that Helm's Creek to the east of the canal, was crossed by a fixed wooden bridge. The swing bridge lasted for 13 years, and was replaced in 1841.

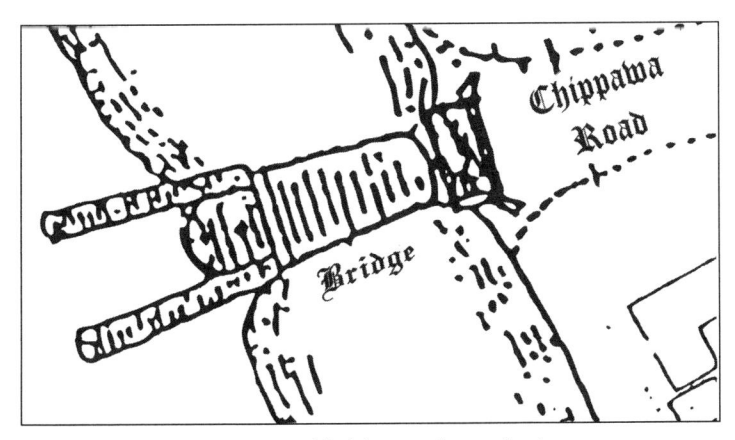

Fig. 17:02   *First canal bridge at Aqueduct.*

In July 1830, a superintendent of the canal company was stationed at Aqueduct to oversee various canal operations in the area. This official was responsible for maintaining the banks and roads in good repair, as well as keeping the canal free of rubbish and timbers. He also erected a tollbooth and was in charge of collecting canal tolls.

Fig. 17:03, combining information from a variety of sources, depicts how the City of Welland, then a shantytown called Aqueduct, may have appeared in the 1830s. Unfortunately, this entire area was obliterated in the 1880s during the excavation of the Third Welland Canal.

And so, the days of Aqueduct, those dozen or so years of Welland's history from 1829, remain shrouded in the mists of time.

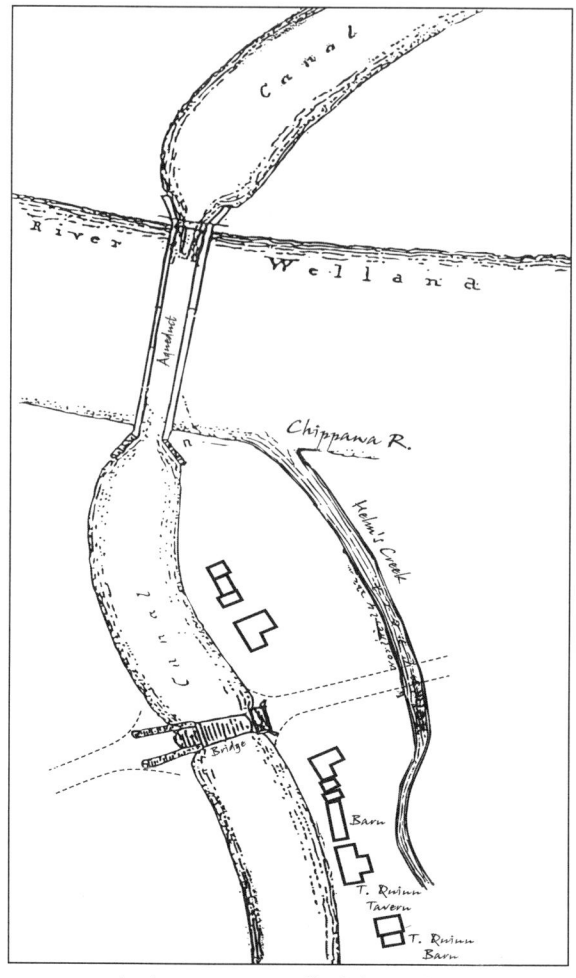

Fig. 17:03   *A shantytown called Aqueduct, 1830s, now the City of Welland.*

Chapter XVIII

On To Port Colborne

During the navigation season of 1830, it became apparent that the route of the canal to Lake Erie was difficult, slow and circuitous. Leaving Port Robinson, vessels upbound had to navigate down the Welland River to Chippawa, then contend with the swift Niagara River current while making their way upstream to Buffalo, and finally sail west on Lake Erie. It therefore became imperative that consideration be given to a more direct passage to the lake.

Various routes south from the Feeder at present-day Welland South were examined in person by the directors of the Welland Canal Company. Gravelly Bay, now Port Colborne, was finally selected in March 1831 as the new Lake Erie entrance to the canal, mainly because that location not only represented the shortest distance to the lake, but also provided an excellent harbour. At Ramey's Bend, the new cut followed a ravine and creek that ran to today's Humberstone, thus requiring less excavation and rock-cutting. This route, visible today at Ramey's Bend and the Main Street weir in Port Colborne, was retained for the subsequent Second and Third Welland Canals, and is depicted in Fig. 18:01.

Accordingly, a loan of £50,000 was obtained from the government of the Province of Upper Canada and work on the new cut soon began. Construction at first was slow, due to rain, difficulty in clearing the land, and a shortage of labour. Furthermore, the work was suddenly halted in 1832 by a catastrophic outbreak of cholera that swept through eastern North America. Merritt reported that the incidence of the scourge among canal labourers, especially at Gravelly Bay, was higher than anywhere else in Canada. Fortunately, with the approach of cold weather, the disease gradually disappeared.

The construction to Lake Erie was not easy, mainly because of the conditions encountered in cutting through the muck and peat of the Wainfleet

Marsh, and then contending with rock at Ramey's Bend.

The headwaters of Lyon's Creek in the Wainfleet Marsh were cut off by the canal extension, and so the creek was carried under the canal through a stone culvert. Slowly, the water level in the marsh receded, and debris collecting in the culvert substantially reduced the water in the stream. Eventually, there was insufficient flow in Lyon's Creek to turn the water wheels at Cook's Mills, and finally, the industries there were closed and abandoned. Due to the Welland Canal, the settlement slowly went into economic recession.

Work on the new cut was accelerated during the fall and winter of 1832, and construction carried on into the following year.

The first transit of the Gravelly Bay extension was made on June 1, 1833 when the schooner *Matilda*, from Oakville, cleared Port Colborne harbour, outbound for Cleveland. By the end of July, 441 schooners, rafts, boats and scows had traversed the canal through the new Lake Erie port.

The First Welland Canal was now complete.

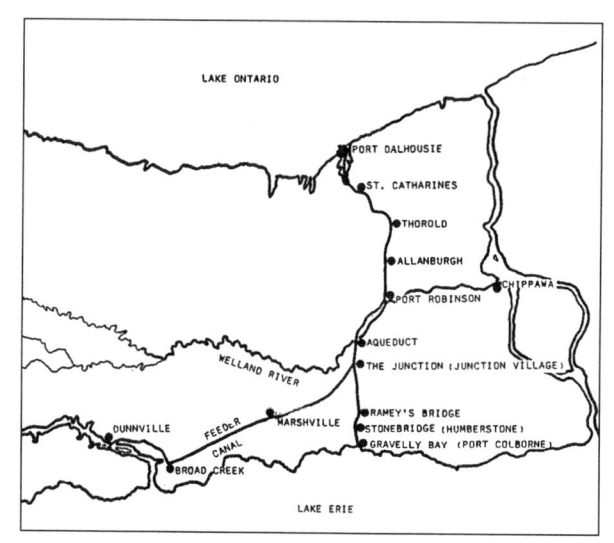

Fig. 18:01   *The First Welland Canal, completed to Lake Erie, 1833.*

Part Four

Merrittsville

Chapter XIX

The Second Welland Canal

By the late 1830s, the First Welland Canal was starting to show its age. Many of the wooden locks, built a dozen years earlier, were in an advanced state of decay; some had begun to settle inwards, thus reducing their effective width for shipping. During the navigation season of 1839, the canal was closed on at least two occasions, for about ten days each time, while some of the locks were undergoing repair. The canal banks also had to be strengthened, since navigation was often obstructed by slippages in the deeper cuts. There were grave concerns that the waterway would soon become impassible.

A number of recommendations for improvement were forthcoming. These included replacing the antiquated wooden locks and aqueduct with stone structures, as well as increasing their size in order to accommodate the increasing use of steam transportation on the Great Lakes. The surface width of the new canal was to be widened to 56 feet, while the bottom width would be increased to 24 feet. It was also proposed that the harbours at both Port Dalhousie and Port Colborne be considerably enlarged and improved, and an entirely new entrance to the canal be dug at Port Dalhousie. (The original entrance to the first canal was in the vicinity of the carousel in present-day Lakeside Park.) The Feeder was to be widened and deepened, and a new channel dug from Stromness to Port Maitland, where a new, large entrance lock was to be constructed.

However, these improvements were beyond the financial means of the privately-owned Welland Canal Company. Accordingly, in 1841, upon the request of the company, the government of the newly created Province of Canada bought out the shareholders of the company, and delegated the responsibility for the waterway to a public Board of Works. (The first chairman of this Board was Hamilton Killaly, after whom Killaly Street in Port Colborne is named.)

Constuction of the Second Welland Canal began in 1842. During the period between 1845 and 1850, the main channel between Welland South and Lake Erie was closed to traffic, and an alternate route to the lake at Port Maitland was provided by the Feeder.

The basic route of the earlier canal was largely unchanged, although significant modifications were made in the area of the aqueduct. The original 40 wooden locks were replaced by 25 new stone structures, including a new lock at the aqueduct to provide access to the canal for navigation along the upper Welland River to Wellandport. Some of these second canal locks may be seen today in the Battle of Beaverdams Park in downtown Thorold, along Bradley Street in Mountain Locks Park in Merritton, and in the former Dick's Creek section of the canal on the east side of Highway 406, near the St. Catharines Golf and Country Club. The second canal lock at Port Maitland, located on the east side of the Grand River, also remains to this day.

Through what is now central Welland, an entirely new channel was excavated for the second canal, since the first aqueduct had to remain open for navigation during the construction of its successor. Whereas the line of the original canal was located along the west side of the fourth canal (the present recreational waterway), this second canal closely followed the east bank of the present downtown channel. These two routes diverged near the foot of today's Raymond Street, and ran beside each other southward to what is now Ontario Road, creating a long, narrow island between the two channels. At Welland South, the new canal connected with the Feeder, while the old waterway terminated in a large pond that provided a water supply for the Feeder's junction lock in that area.

The two canals were crossed by separate bridges at Main Street. A new swing bridge over the second canal was constructed at the corner of Main Street and today's King Street. Later in the 1850s, when the original waterway was closed to navigation and the wooden aqueduct dismantled, the swing bridge over the first canal was replaced by a fixed span. Between the two bridges was the narrow island referred to above.

Fig. 19:01   *Second canal swing bridge, 1840s.*

Only a small length of Helm's Creek remained open after the construction of the second canal. For the most part, the creek was carried by a culvert under the new waterway, and continued as a drain on the east side of the canal to a pond on the present site of Merritt Park. The remainder of the creek south to Ontario Road was absorbed into the line of the second canal, and about 1845, the bridge carrying the Chippawa Road over the creek was dismantled.

Fig. 19:02 *Fixed span replacing first canal swing bridge.*

A new stone lock was constructed at the junction of the Feeder and the main channel. Today, this lock sits dry, buried up to its coping stone, and may be seen in the overgrown, ill-kept parkette, hidden near the west end of the Broadway Street bridge. What little that is visible of this structure is shown in Fig. 19:03.

Fig. 19:03   *The abandoned Feeder Canal lock in Welland South.*

The central area of present-day Welland, as it was in the early 1850s, after the completion of the second canal and aqueduct, is depicted in Fig. 19:04. The new aqueduct and the two bridges, as well as the truncated Helm's Creek, and the demolished first aqueduct, are indicated.

These changes to the canal system in the area of the aqueducts were to have profound and lasting significance to the form of urban development of what would eventually become the City of Welland.

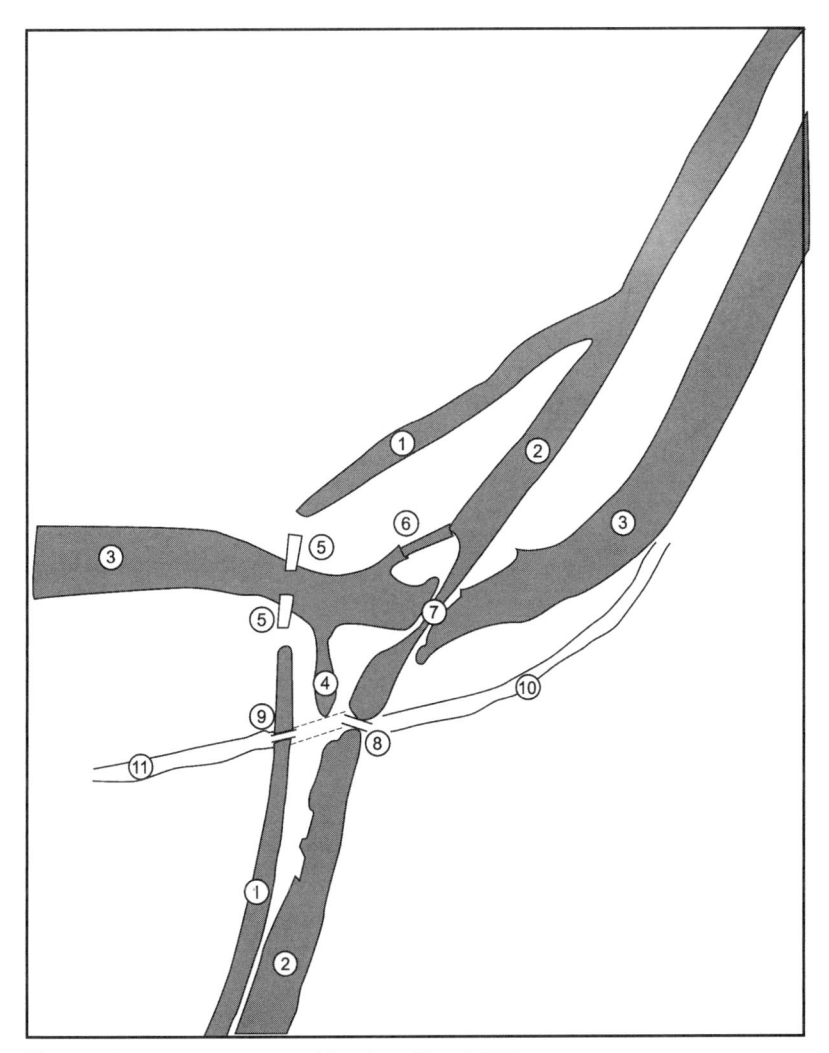

Fig. 19:04   *Merrittsville, 1850s.*

Legend

1) First Welland Canal
2) Second Welland Canal
3) Welland River
4) Helm's Creek
5) Dismantled First Canal aqueduct, converted to storehouses
6) Canal lock to river
7) Second canal aqueduct
8) Swing bridge, second canal
9) Fixed bridge, first canal
10) Chippawa Road
11) Road to Wellandport

Chapter XX

The Second Aqueduct

As mentioned, the route of the Second Welland Canal, for most of the waterway, was not significantly different from that of its predecessor. However, in the area of what is today central Welland, an entirely new channel had to be excavated, since it was necessary that the first canal aqueduct remain in service during the construction of its replacement.

In February 1841, the Board of Works received plans for a new aqueduct from Samuel Power, a canal engineer, and in May directed Power to advertise the work and to prepare tenders. The Board of Works recommended that the aqueduct be built "in a permanent manner of stone," that it not interfere with the passage of water in the river, and that a lock connecting the river and the canal be constructed upstream from the aqueduct. Estimates of the cost of the aqueduct ranged from £16,000 to £18,000, depending on the final depth of the structure. The new aqueduct was to be 316 feet long and 45 feet wide, with a depth of 10 feet.

However, work did not get under way very quickly. It was not until February 1844 that the contract for the construction of the second aqueduct was finally awarded to the firm of Zimmerman and McCullough. (A few years later, Zimmerman erected the first bridge across the Niagara Gorge, and went on to become a successful banker, among other ventures.)

The second canal was officially opened on May 21, 1845, but as the stone aqueduct was not complete, navigation was required to still use the original canal channel and the wooden aqueduct.

In February 1846, Power reported that the foundation for the new aqueduct had been laid, the supporting piers built and much of the centering columns framed and in place. He described the aqueduct as the most important, difficult and expensive project on the canal line, and that "great exertions" would be required to complete the work by 1847. It was noted that no arrangements had yet been made for the construction of the nearby lock to the Welland River.

In July 1846, Power was replaced as canal superintendant by Samuel Keefer.

During the summer of that year, the contractor Zimmerman complained that it would not be possible for him to complete the aqueduct at the tendered price, and that the work would have to be suspended at the most critical construction stage, before the four arches were closed, leaving the whole weight of the structure resting on the centre columns.

In October, a new contract was awarded to Zimmerman and work resumed. The arches were closed and the finishing stonework was carried up to the top of the arches. Large quantities of stone had been provided for the parapets. Later that month, work was again suspended by the Board of Works due to financial constraints.

A constant worry was the condition of the first canal aqueduct, which by now had been in use for 18 years. Keefer was concerned that a delay in completion of the new aqueduct could jeopardize navigation, since it was impossible to know how long the old wooden structure would last, and so, later that year, the old superstructure was replaced. Keefer hoped that this stopgap work would keep the original aqueduct operational until the replacement was completed.

In 1847, construction resumed. The magnificent stone blocks for the parapets were dressed at their Queenston quarry, and delivered finished to the construction site. Keefer expressed the hope that the aqueduct would be finished that year and in use for the 1848 navigation season. However, this was not to be.

Construction continued through 1848. Concrete was laid for the bottom flooring, and work was completed to the height of the coping, although this was not bolted down, as there was some uncertainty as to the final depth of water in the aqueduct. In July, a steam dredge was sent to remove the protecting cofferdams holding back the water at the job site. Later, in October, a still unhappy Keefer complained that Zimmerman seemed to be in no hurry to finish the aqueduct, even though the work was so close to completion. But the superintendant also indicated that he had brought no pressure on the contractor, as the government was very concerned about expenditures.

Finally, after two more years of work, the immense project was completed, and the Board of Works was able to announce that the stone aqueduct and the lock to the river were ready for the spring opening of the 1851 navigation season.

This aqueduct still stands in downtown Welland, and is a testimony to the outstanding craftmanship of over 150 years ago. Unfortunately, the arches referred to above are buried below ground, but the magnificent stonemasonry of the parapets is visible to this day.

Fig. 20:01 *The Second Welland Canal aqueduct in operation.*

Fig. 20:01 depicts the second aqueduct in operation almost 150 years ago. In contrast, the photograph by Master Photographer Thies Bogner of Welland, reproduced as Fig. 20:02, shows this landmark as it is today.

Fig. 20:02   *The Second Welland Canal aqueduct today.*

The river lock, situated at the foot of Lock Street, played an important role in the significant lumber trade that was carried on at a number of locations on the Welland River upstream and west of the canal. Cut timber was moved overland to such ports as O'Reilly's Bridge, Beckett's Bridge and Wellandport, where the logs were then assembled into rafts, often for transport to the growing industrial centre at Buffalo, and even on to Lockport. Tugs had begun to replace the poling of these rafts to transport the lumber; however, the clearance under the new aqueduct was too low to permit the passage of these tugs. Thus eastbound timber was pushed under the aqueduct, the tug would lock up into the canal and proceed to Port Robinson, then lock back down into the river, and return to the east side of the aqueduct to collect its floating cargo.

The second aqueduct and the Feeder lock in Welland South are all that remain today of the early canal heritage of the City of Welland, and merit permanent recognition and preservation.

Chapter XXI

Junction Village

Aqueduct was not the only community within the boundaries of present-day Welland that came into being due to the Welland Canal. A small settlement arose on the east side of the canal at the junction of the Feeder and the Port Colborne extension, and was called, appropriately, The Junction, or just Junction. (This should not be confused with today's Welland Junction or Dain City.)

Junction, sometimes referred to as Helmsport, Port Hellems or Hellemsport, originated in the area of today's Canalbank Street. The settlement was named after John A. Hellems, who had fought at Lundy's Lane in the War of 1812. The Hellems farm, settled in 1804, extended from Denistoun Street east to Plymouth Road, and from Lincoln Street south to Ontario Road. Hellems also operated a wharf on the west side of the canal, south of the junction with the Feeder. As early as 1840, Hellems served as a Justice of the Peace, at a time when work on the canal brought a large number of lawless men into this area.

Junction came into being in the mid-1840s when Hellems developed and sold a number of village lots along the east side of Canalbank Street, which in those days was called Main Street. Other buildings in the settlement were located on present-day Ontario Road, near the canal.

According to *Smith's Canadian Gazetteer* of 1846, Junction had a population of about 60 inhabitants, and the settlement boasted two stores, two taverns and a blacksmith shop, as well as a tailor and a shoemaker. One tavern, at the north end of the village's Main Street, was owned by James Tuft; the other publican was James Boyd, and his tavern was nearer the corner of Ontario Road, on property purchased from John Hellems in 1848.

A prominent feature of Junction was the Traveller's Home, a 22-room hotel built in 1848 by James Tuft, the tavern owner. (It could well be that the

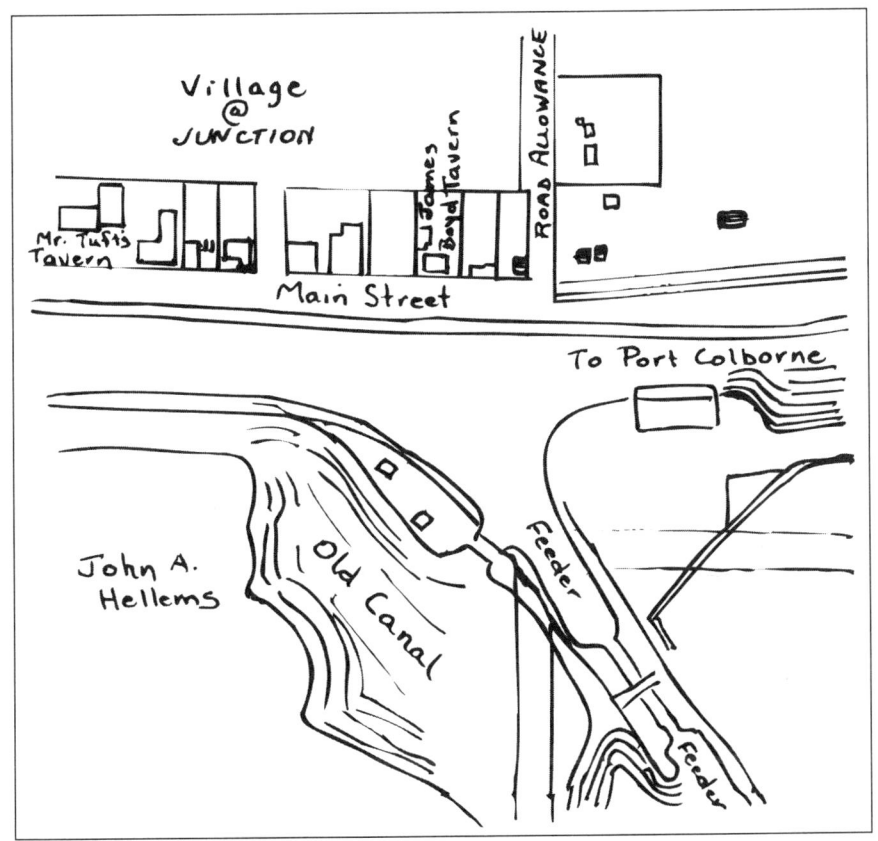

Fig. 21:01   *The Junction, or Helmsport, 1840s.*

tavern and the hotel were the same establishment.) The structure was located on Canalbank Street, near the present railway underpass. The hotel boasted a large ballroom on the second floor where weekly square dances were held. After Tuft's death, the hotel was managed by Sarah Jane McCabe, and then by her daughter, Addie. In later years, the building was known as the McCabe House, and was demolished in the early 1970s.

Inasmuch as Tufts built two homes for members of his family on Ontario Road, it may well be that Junction led to the development of the commercial and residential area on Ontario Road between King and Canalbank Streets, and at the south end of King Street.

Chapter XXII
Concession 5, Lots 24 and 25

When surveyed in the late 1700s and early 1800s, most of the townships in what is now southern Ontario were divided into concessions. These numbered east-west tracts of land are separated by concession lines 1¼ miles apart, and eventually these lines became allowances for roads. The base line for the surveys of Crowland Township was Townline Road, and the concession lines became Ontario Road, Lincoln Street, East Main Street, and then Shisler, Young, Carl and Biggar Roads. The concessions were further divided into lots of 100 acres each; these lots also were numbered.

As noted, the original settlement of Aqueduct was located on what is today the west side of Welland. Prior to the construction of the Second Welland Canal and the second aqueduct, there was no urban presence on the east side of the canal.

The central area of the east side of Welland was originally Lots 24 and 25 of the Fifth Concession of Crowland Township. These two lots extend from the original East Main Street survey line south to Lincoln Street, and from near King Street to about the railway right-of-way at Atlas Steels. The dividing line between the two lots is Hellems Avenue. The west side of the city's central area is Lots 26 and 27, which are separated by Denistoun Street. These lots are depicted in Fig. 22:01.

Lots 24 and 25 were granted by the Crown in 1796 to Captain Thomas Welch, a retired British officer and political appointee. Later, in 1806, Robert Hamilton purchased the lots as part of a 388-acre parcel of land that included most of central Welland. Hamilton, born in Scotland in 1753, was a prosperous Queenston merchant and one of the most influential commercial and political figures in the early history of the Niagara area. (Hamilton's second son, the Hon. George Hamilton moved to the Burlington Bay area in 1812, where he founded the City of Hamilton.) By the end of the 1700s, Robert Hamilton had amassed a personal fortune, mainly by providing supplies to

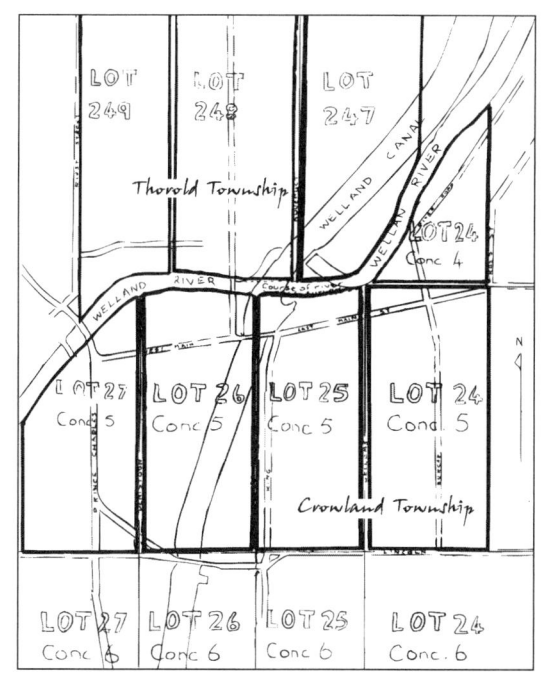

Fig. 22:01

the fur trade and to the military. Hamilton was undoubtedly the chief land speculator in early Upper Canada and acquired in excess of 130,000 acres of land, of which 30,000 acres were in the Niagara Peninsula.

Subsequent to Hamilton's death in 1809, ownership of large tracts of this land in today's downtown Welland changed hands through a complex series of transactions, mainly within the same family. In 1836, Duncan McFarland, of Port Robinson, and John Donaldson, of Mount Healy in Haldimand County, purchased the east half of Lot 25; some years later, most of the west half of Lot 25 was acquired by Jacob Griffith, after whom Griffith Street is named.

(McFarland had operated a store at Allanburg, but later moved to Port Robinson where, in 1829, he became the village's first postmaster. Donaldson was the founder of Mount Healy, a Grand River hamlet that has largely disappeared over the intervening years.)

It is an interesting insight into the 19th-century legal system to note that some 18 years after purchasing these lands, McFarland and Donaldson were concerned that in one of the family transactions referred to above, a Mrs. Mary Ann McQueen had, in 1834, not complied with the statutes then in effect in Upper Canada that limited the right of married women to sell their real estate. To protect their interests, McFarland and Donaldson obtained from a daughter of Mrs. McQueen clear title to the land for the price of five shillings (about one dollar.) Furthermore, in this 1856 deal, the married daughter required the consent of her husband to finalize the transaction.

It is important to emphasize that these land transfers were rural transactions, and that none involved the sale or purchase of a small enough parcel of land to be considered an urban lot.

This situation was soon to change.

CHAPTER XXIII

MERRITTSVILLE APPEARS

As related, construction of the Second Welland Canal began in 1842, with work on the stone aqueduct getting under way two years later. It is possible that the inhabitants of Aqueduct considered that the somewhat prosaic name of their community did not do justice to the majestic structure that was taking form in their hamlet.

A contemporary account in the *St. Catharines Journal* reported:

> the inhabitants anticipating future growth.... called a meeting.... and gave to the village its present name, the mover saying the Welland Canal had its Dunnville, Maitland, Colborne, Robinson, Allanburg, etc., while he who was justly called the Father of the Canal had not received the honour due him, insomuch as his name had not found a place in any of those villages which had arisen from his wisdom, it was.... resolved that the place should be called Merrittville.

The proposal from the meeting was forwarded to the Niagara District Council, the body responsible for local government in the peninsula at that time, and the change of name was approved.

The *St. Catharines Journal* of November 28, 1844 reported:

> Thursday, November 14.
>
> On a motion of Mr.[Dexter] D'Everardo, and seconded by Mr.[Duncan] McFarland, the village at the new aqueduct of the Welland Canal was christened "MERRITTVILLE", and a copy of the resolution

was directed to be transmitted to the Township Clerks of Thorold and Crowland, with instructions to them to place a copy of the name upon their respective Town Books.

Thus, the hamlet gave suitable recognition to William Hamilton Merritt, and the name Aqueduct, after 15 years, ceased to be.

(It should be noted that Merrittsville is sometimes referred to as Merrittville, such as seen above, or as spelled in the Merrittville Highway. However, Merrittsville is the name most frequently found in official documents, and is the form that has been used throughout this work.)

The coming of the second aqueduct, while apparently giving rise to civic pride, nevertheless did cause concern in some quarters. In February 1848 the Niagara District Council petitioned the provincial Legislative Assembly to take steps to improve the flow of the Welland River, since:

> .... in consequence of the stagnant nature of the water of the River Welland.... which will be made more so by the arches of the Aqueduct.... being below the surface of the water, disease is engendered and continues to increase yearly, insomuch that for the past few years, the majority of the inhabitants living along its banks.... have been confined to their beds for the most part of the summer and fall. Such were the consequences last year that in the Townships of Wainfleet and Gainsboro, there was scarcely a house in which there were not two or three laid on sick beds during the whole summer, and some of these heads of large families.

Merrittsville's original roadway through what is today downtown Welland was the Chippawa Road, which crossed the first canal and Helms Creek, and then followed the east and south bank of the Welland River to Chippawa. When Crowland Township was initially surveyed, the road from Cook's

Mills between Concessions 4 and 5 originally followed a straight line directly west to the river, and there intersected the Chippawa Road. A small part of that original concession line roadway remains today as a short section of Dorothy Street, behind the parking lot of the Liquor Control Board outlet.

In order to provide a more direct line to the new swing bridge over the second canal, the concession road was re-aligned westwardly with a bend near the present railway tracks at Atlas Steels, and now led directly to the new bridge. The road was renamed Main Street, and the old road allowance was closed by a township by-law. Main Street (now both East and West Main Streets), the parallel Division Street and intersecting Cross Street, became the nucleus, and the eventual commercial centre of Merrittsville.

The divergence of these two roadways has given rise to a number of different street and lot alignments in downtown Welland. The earliest lots offered for sale on East Main Street near the bridge were squared to the new Main Street, while parcels of land that were sold later were aligned with the original concession road.

Similarly, some of the oldest streets in the city such as Dorothy, Division, and Grove Streets on the east side, and Bald Street and Maple Avenue on the west side, are parallel to Main Street. Other streets are laid out north and south, and thus are perpendicular to the concessions.

Some streets were aligned with both roadways, and this explains why bends are encountered on King, Burgar, Grove, Randolph and Griffith Streets, and why Cross Street and Hellems Avenue are not parallel to each other.

These diverging street lines, and the original Chippawa Road concession line, are indicated on Fig. 23:01.

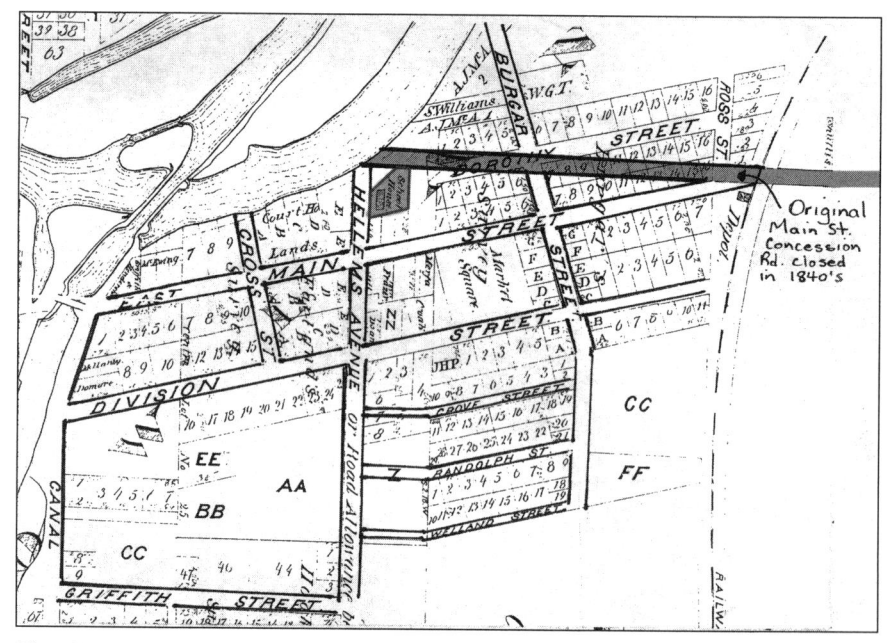

Fig. 23:01   *The original Main Street is highlighted in grey.*

Chapter XXIV

The Village

Like Aqueduct, little description of Merrittsville has survived to this day.

However, a rather unflattering account of the village appeared in the *St. Catharines Journal* of January 22, 1850. According to the writer, Merrittsville was situated

> on each side of the Chippawa.... somewhat repulsive in first appearance, on account of the number of temporary buildings erected by canalers and others connected with the public works, but as soon as these are completed, the shanties will give rise to better buildings, and the place will make quite a different appearance.

Smith's Canadian Gazetteer noted that in 1846, Merrittsville boasted about 100 inhabitants, with five stores, three taverns, two tailors and two shoemakers.

As described earlier, little urban presence had been evident initially on the east side of the canals. However, with the construction of the second canal, and especially the second aqueduct, Merrittsville slowly, and then more rapidly in the mid-1850s, began to assume the appearance of an urban community. By 1851, the population of the village had increased to about 250, as noted by Mackay's *Canada Directory* of that year. Mackay's listing for Merrittsville in given in Appendix "B", and provides insight into the growing business activity of the community.

The first recorded sale of a village lot in today's east-side downtown Welland, was to Robert Ramsden, a carpenter, who, in May 1845, purchased a quarter-acre parcel of land on the north side of Main Street, near the new swing bridge. Then Duncan McFarland and John Donaldson, the owners of the east half of Lot 25, had a portion of their property surveyed and subdivided into 37 lots on Main, Cross and Division Streets. Subsequently, Jacob Griffith, who as noted previously, had acquired the west half of Lot 25, began about 1851 to sell 12 village lots from part of his property on Main Street, near the new canal.

Griffith built the first house in present-day downtown Welland, as early as 1843, on a site on Canal Street (today's King Street) now occupied by For The Love of Books. Another homeowner in this area was Eli Mead, who had purchased a large lot from Griffith at the corner of Canal and Division Streets.

Other developments soon followed. Between 1855 and 1859, Thomas Burgar subdivided his farm fronting on the Welland River into three parcels of lots. (The Burgar family home is today's Rinderland's Dining Rooms.) About the same time, Nathan T. Fitch opened up a parcel of land that extended along both sides of Canal Street, south to Lincoln Street.

The west side of the village also witnessed rapid development. In 1853, James Shotwell surveyed a plot of land between Shotwell and Aqueduct Streets that extended from Church Street almost to the river. The following year, William Bald subdivided that part of his farm located between West Main Street and Jane Street (now Maple Avenue) from the first canal west to Denistoun Street. Similarly, in 1857, Jesse Stoner and Moses Betts opened two other parcels of land in the West Main Street area.

Merrittsville was on its way.

Fig. 24:01

The urban growth of the village in the mid-1850s is illustrated by various development plans of Merrittsville, which are reproduced in Appendix "A". The location and time sequence of these real estate activities are depicted in Fig. 24:02.

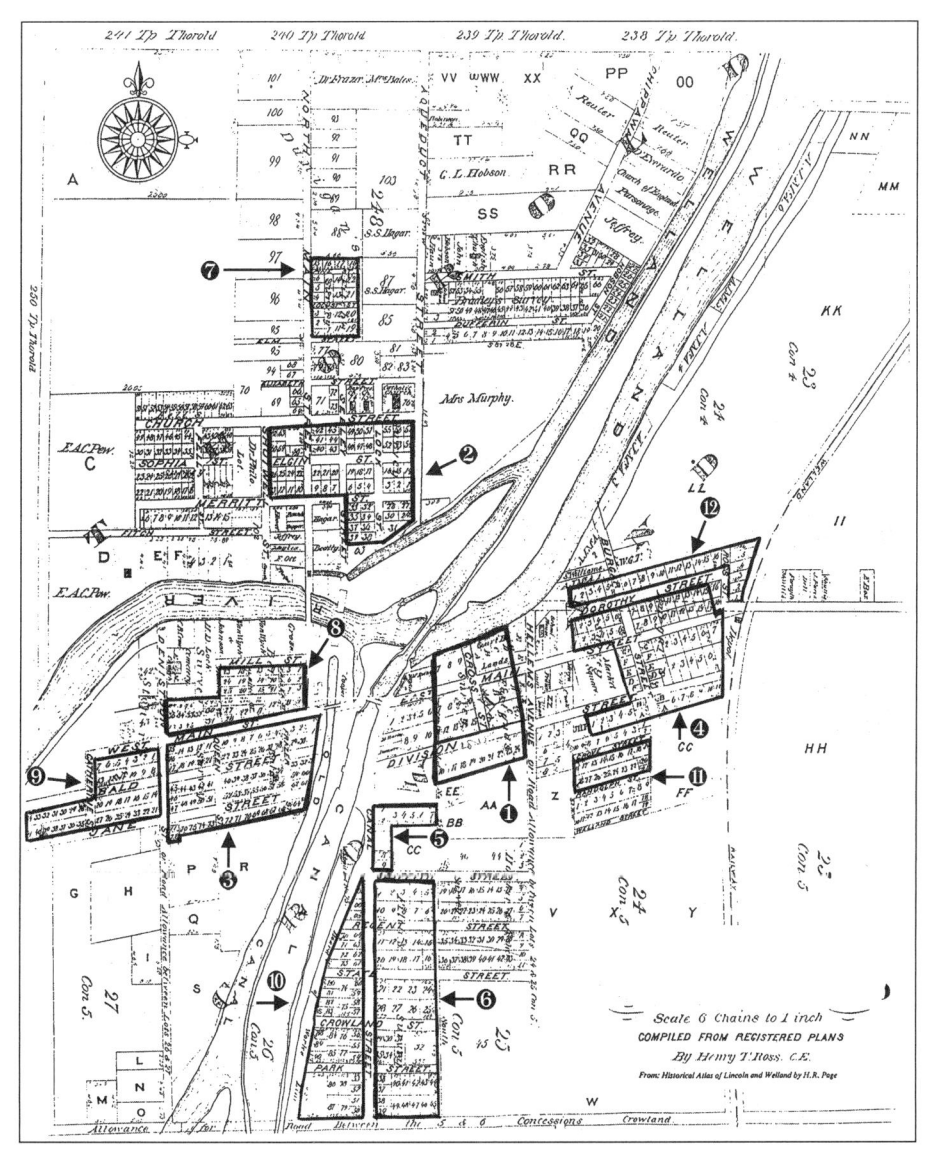

Fig. 24:02   The development of Merrittsville.

Legend

1) 1845 - McFarland & Donaldson
2) 1853 - James Shotwell
3) 1854 - William A. Bald
4) 1855 - Thomas Burgar
5) 1856 - Jacob Griffith
6) 1856 - N.T. Fitch
7) 1856 - N.T. Fitch
8) 1857 - Moses Betts
9) 1857 - Jessie Stoner
10) 1858 - N.T. Fitch
11) 1858 - Thomas Burgar
12) 1859 - Thomas Burgar

Chapter XXV

Industry and Commerce

Mention has been made that there are no reports of any mills being located at Aqueduct, in spite of the 16-foot difference in water levels between the original canal and the Welland River. However, with the coming of Merrittsville and the second canal, a milling industry began to appear in the village.

In the fall of 1847, the first grist mill, the Welland Flouring Mills, was established by two natives of New York State, Thomas Dunlop and Ebenezer Seeley, who became involved in a number of enterprises near the canals. Their mill was located on the north bank of the river, a short distance west of North Main Street (today's Niagara Street). To power the mill, water was drawn from the old canal near the aqueduct, and fed through a millpond and raceway to the mill's waterwheel. The partners paid an annual lease of £54 to the Board of Works for these water rights. This mill was destroyed by fire in 1886.

MERRITTVILLE MILLS

THE Subscribers offer for sale for Cash, or in exchange for Saw Logs, or Grain of all kinds, at their mills in the village of Merrittville—

Lumber, rough, planed or planed & matched Shingles, Salt, Flour, Corn Meal, Buck-wheat Flour, Mill Feed, &c;

CUSTOM GRINDING done with despatch, and warranted well done. DUNLAP & SEELEY.

Goods of most kinds can be had in this village as as good terms as at any other place in the neighborhood. Wool Carding and Cloth Dressing also done here. Merrittville, Nov. 1852

Fig. 25:01

Dunlop and Seeley also operated two other mills north of the river. Sheep-raising in the Short Hills and Crowland Township led in 1850 to the establishment of their woolen factory, which was situated between the grist mill and the river. Their sawmill was located east of North Main Steet and obtained the required water supply from the millpond. Today, a small parkette adjacent to the north end of the Niagara Street bridge occupies the site of the sawmill. These mills are located in Fig. 25:02, which also depicts the dammed-up first aqueduct, as well as the millpond and raceway to the mills.

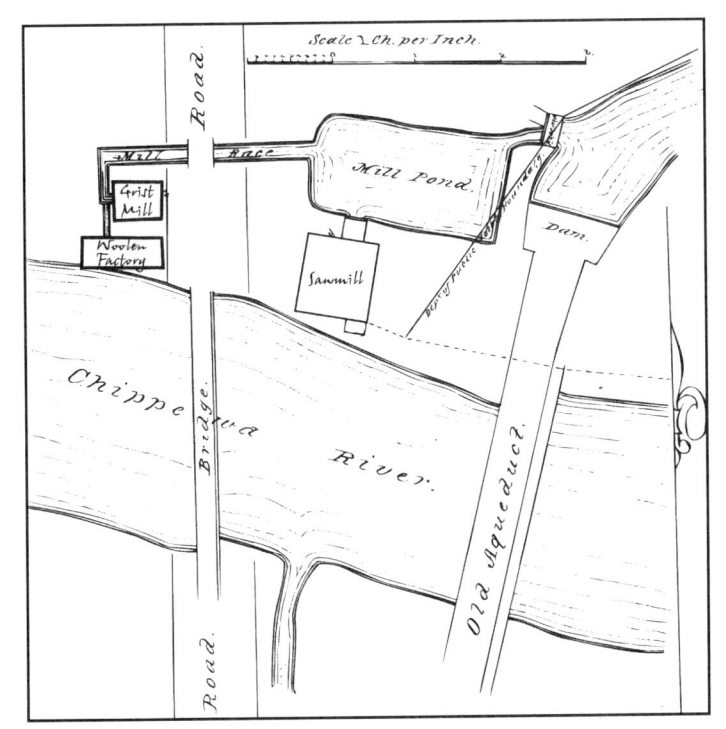

Fig. 25:02   *Riverside mills of Dunlop and Seeley.*

Seeley was involved in a number of other enterprises near the canal. His second sawmill was located between the river and the canal bridge, and derived its water power from a flume that connected with a raceway south of the river. In addition, after the wooden aqueduct was dismantled, Seeley converted the north and south stone approaches of the old structure into storehouses, which were accessible to shipping that could lock down into the river from the new canal. Another storehouse was constructed by Seeley at the corner of North and West Main Streets, where Bogner Photography and Gallery is now located.

The two grist mills were not particularly large operations, as it was reported that their sales in 1851 were only £1,500 and they employed less than ten people.

The fact that Dunlop and Seeley were Americans created some controversy, and a letter critical of Seeley appeared in a St. Catharines newspaper in 1850. Seeley had been granted rights to draw water from the Welland Canal for his

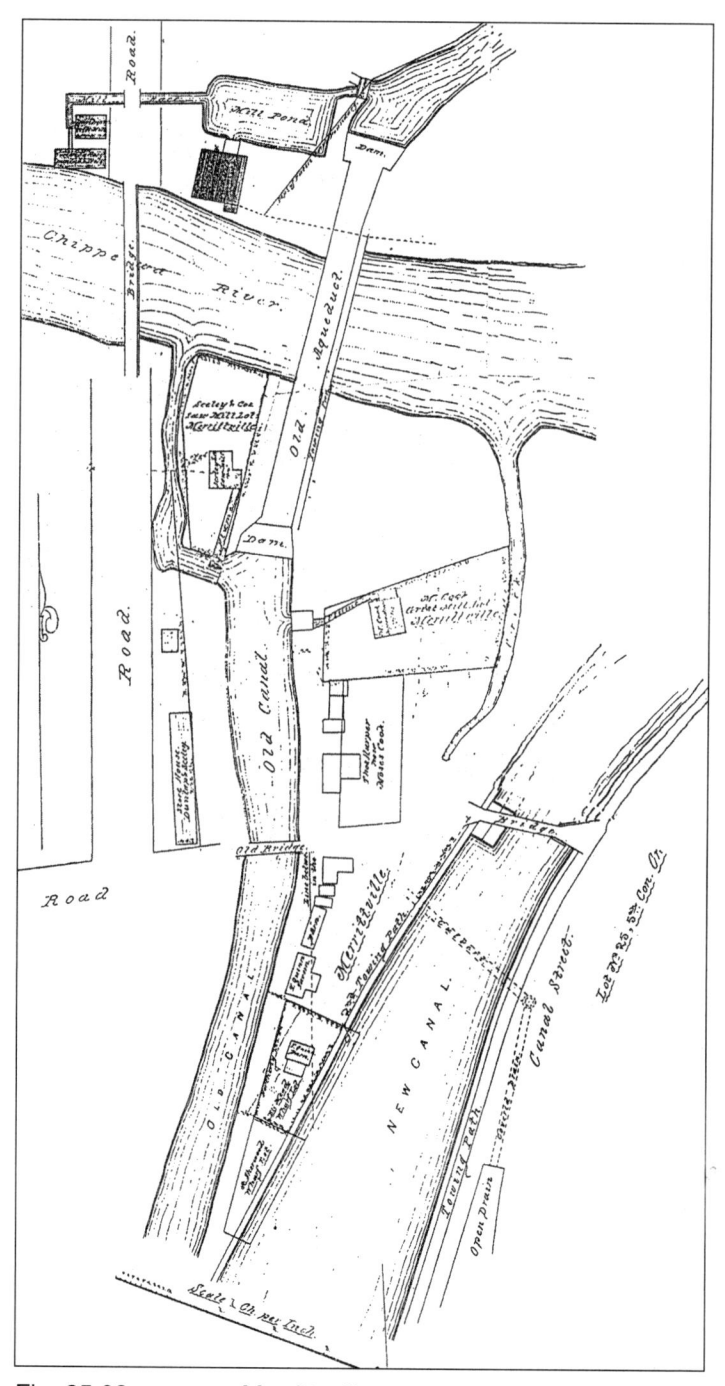

Fig. 25:03   Merrittsville, c.1858.
Many of the commercial enterprises of the village are depicted above.

mill, and the writer complained that Seeley was taking his profits out of the country. In rebuttal, another correspondent, citing the mill-owner's investment in Merrittsville, replied that since 1847, Seeley had "expended between $35 and $40,000 for land, timber, labour, teams, tools and provisions of all kinds."

About 1850, Moses Cook also built a gristmill, which was located between the two canals, near the river. The mill was powered by water through a flume that was drawn from the old canal, after the dam was constructed across the approaches to the wooden aqueduct. Like Seeley's aqueduct warehouses, Cook's mill was so situated that a vessel could be locked from the canal into the river and brought up to his mill, where the boat could be loaded with flour, and then proceed directly to Montreal or other eastern markets.

An early description of Merrittsville indicates that one of the two grist mills had "three run of stones," and that one of the sawmills boasted "two single saws, three circular saws, and a planing machine." The account continues: "the resident population scarcely numbers one hundred and fifty, but the labourers casually employed on the canal will raise the numbers to nearly three hundred and fifty."

By 1853, Merrittsville's industries had increased to include a brewery, a rope yard, a lath factory, a pottery, a pail factory and a tannery.

Another early industry, the Hooker Brick and Tile Works, was founded by Thaddeus W. Hooker, a native of Vermont, who came to Merrittsville in 1855 and obtained a contract to manufacture bricks for the construction of the new Welland County Court House. The brickworks were located near the present Welland Tennis Club, on a 30-acre plot which Hooker purchased in 1856 from William A. Bald. Some traces of the brickworks may still be seen in the field behind the Convent of the Sisters of Sacred Heart on Edward Street. Hooker manufactured brick for the majority of such buildings erected in Merrittsville and the surrounding area, including some of the oldest homes on the west side of present-day Welland. The Hooker family residence, naturally of brick construction, was built in 1855, and remains to this day at 33 Maple Avenue.

One of the busiest places in Merrittsville was Sherwood's warehouse and wharf, on the west bank of the new canal. Sherwood's lot was south of the Main Street bridge, and backed onto the old canal. Cordwood, stavebolts and shingles were the main products handled. A second wharf, operated by Eli Mead, was adjacent to the Sherwood wharf. Thomas Quinn's barn, referred to in Chapter XVII, had earlier been located on Mead's wharf lot. These businesses were torn down during the construction of the third canal in the 1880s, and like most of Welland's early heritage, are no longer even a memory.

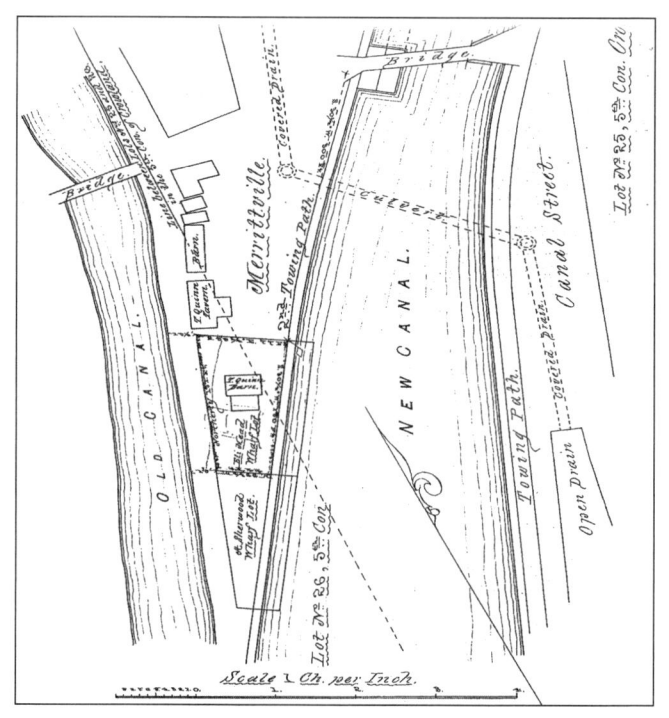

Fig. 25:04   *Sherwood and Mead wharf lots.*
*Also shown are Thomas Quinn's tavern and barn,
as well as other buildings from the days of Aqueduct, along the first canal.*

In August 1849, Thomas Burgar was appointed the first postmaster of Merrittsville. This appointment lagged far behind the establishment of post offices in other small communities along the canal, indicating the initial slow development of Aqueduct and Merrittsville. The location of Burgar's post office is shown in Fig. 25:05. Today, the site of the original post office is 9 East Main Street.

The *St. Catharines Journal* reported in 1850 that three "Merchant shops" were located in Merrittsville, as well as three houses called Inns, that were "mainly erected not for the travelling public, but for the sale of ardent spirits." One of these watering holes was named the Merrittsville House.

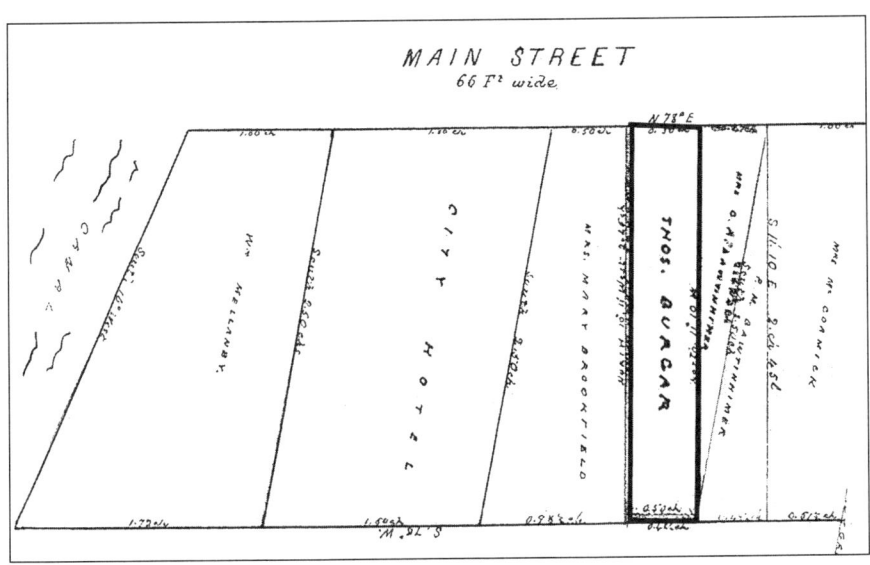

Fig. 25:05   The location of Thomas Burgar's Post Office is shown above.

A "Business Directory of Canada West," which appears in *Canada: Past, Present and Future*, by W. H. Smith, and published in 1851, lists the three merchants as Thomas Finn, Elijah Schooley and A.W. Shrigley. The directory also includes Moses Cook, a miller, Dunlop and Seeley, millers and lumber merchants, and Francis Ellenwood, a woolen manufacturer.

The first newspaper in the area was the *Welland Herald*, the forerunner of today's *Tribune*. The *Herald*, first published in 1854, was not printed in Merrittsville but rather in Fonthill. Local publication had to await the coming of the Village of Welland.

A further sign of progress was, that on June 20, 1855, the locks and bridges of the canal were, for the first time, illuminated by gas lamps.

By the mid-1850s, Merrittsville's population had grown significantly to some 700 to 800 inhabitants, and this progress was reflected by the increase in the number and variety of commercial enterprises that the village was able to support. The diversity of this business activity is demonstrated in *The Canada Directory*, compiled in 1857 by John Lovell. This directory lists the commercial and professional complement of almost every municipality and location in what is today Ontario, including Merrittsville. The increase in the village's commerce from the 1851 reference given above, is truly remarkable. Not only did the village support butchers, grocers and a tailor, but also more esoteric occupations were represented, including a perfumer and a rectifier. Lovell's complete entry for Merrittsville is reproduced in Appendix "C".

Two of Welland's longest operating retail establishments were founded during the Merrittsville years. Richard Morwood, who was born in 1831 in Oneida County, N.Y., began a mercantile business on West Main Street in 1856, and was able to supply his customers with "almost everything from a paper of pins to the most costly dress goods." In later years, the R. Morwood Company was largely a hardware operation, but the firm's reputation of being able to satisfy any customer's request continued throughout three generations. The store was destroyed by fire on a cold and windy Friday night in December 1968.

Fig. 25:06

Another venerable firm was that of D. McCaw and Sons. This properous shoemaking and retail store was founded by Daniel McCaw, who emigrated from Ireland, first to Port Colborne and then to Merrittsville. In 1851, he purchased one of the first village lots from McFarland and Donaldson, and began business as a shoemaker, which McCaw expanded in 1867 into a retail shoe store. The business was situated at the present Canada Trust location on the corner of East Main and Cross Streets, and also like Morwood's, continued to be operated by three generations of the same family. McCaw's Shoe Store was closed in the 1980s with the retirement of Douglas McCaw, grandson of the founder.

Fig. 25:07

(It may be of interest to note that decimal currency was introduced into the Province of Canada in 1858. (The original coinage included twenty cent pieces, but not quarters.) However, due to a scarcity of the new currency, retail trade in Merrittsvile was conducted in both pounds and dollars for some time.)

TWENTY CENT
VICTORIA
DATE   NO. MINTED
1858 750,000

By the late 1850s, Merrittsville had become one of the leading business centres of the Niagara Peninsula.

Chapter XXVI

The Bridge on the River Welland

In the early days of Aqueduct and Merrittsville, there was no bridge in the hamlet over the Welland River. The reason for this may have been that the settlement was not incorporated and, therefore, had no municipal government. Furthermore, as Merrittsville was situated on both sides of the river, the responsibility for a crossing was divided between Crowland and Thorold Townships, and so nothing was done. It is likely that the only passage over the river was afforded by the 12-foot-wide towpath on the east side of the first aqueduct. It is also probable that North Main Street (Niagara Street) did not exist.

However, in 1848, an agreement for the sale of land from Smith Shotwell to Ebenezer Seeley provided for a roadway between Thorold Township's Chippawa Road (today's Colbeck Drive and Merritt Street) and Seeley's mill on the north side of the river.

The following year, Crowland Township Council passed a motion "to assist in building a bridge over the River Welland in Merrrittsville," and apportioned five pounds to John Hellems for the work. This structure was soon completed, and the *St. Catharines Journal* of February 28, 1850 was able to report:

> The inhabtants [of Merrittsville] have erected a good bridge across the Chippawa on the west side of the Aqueduct on the direct line of the road from St. Catharines to Port Colborne, which is now a tolerable good road, a saving of about 5 miles between the two places over the old road by Port Robinson.

It would seem, however, that further work was necessary. In 1851, the Crowland Township Council passed "An Act to Remove Obstructions from a Certain Road in Crowland Township." This act stipulated that:

> It is necessary and expedient to open the Road leading from the Bridge across the River Welland at the Village of Merrittville to the Road known as the River Road [now West Main Street] and to remove obstructions therefrom.

On December 18, 1850, John Hellems chaired a meeting in the Merrittsville schoolhouse to improve this road by proposing the formation of a company to build a plank road from St. Catharines to Merrittsville. It was moved:

> that great advantage must accrue to the town of St. Catharines and the village of Merrittsville by the construction of a Plank and Macadamized Road between the above places, opening as it will, a direct line of communication between Lakes Erie and Ontario, affording a double market to the productions of one of the finest sections of agricultural country in Canada.

It was further moved that the meeting form itself into a joint stock company, to be called the St. Catharines and Merrittsville Turnpike Company. Two years later, the St. Catharines Town Council supported the venture by voting to take £3,000 of stock in the company. Later contracts stipulated that the work be done in sections of one mile each, with the first four miles south from St. Catharines to be macadamized, and the remainder planked.

Plank roads were built of logs placed crosswise along a roadbed, and in spite of their roughness, these corduroy surfaces were a vast improvement over the mud holes that, all too often, were the roads of that time. The private companies that constructed such roads, of course, extracted tolls from those travelling on their right of ways.

Fig. 26:01   *A typical plank road.*

The *St. Catharines Journal* of November 25, 1852 reported:

> We travelled over this road a few weeks ago.... and we must say that the country through which the road passes is one of great interest, and the amount of travel with which it will intersect is very considerable. The fact also of Merrittville being now the place selected for the site of the county buildings, will add considerably to the importance of this road.

Some early plans of Merrittsville describe North Main Street as the "Plank Road." Today, the turnpike toll road constructed by the stock company is known as the Merrittville Highway.

Until the mid-1930s, North Main Street ended at Thorold Road. There was no Niagara Street beyond that point. A traveller to St. Catharines was therefore obliged to turn right from North Main Street onto Thorold Road, and then turn left onto Aqueduct Street.

A further improvement to the river bridge came a few years later. In December 1856, the Welland County Council Committee of Roads and Bridges moved that the Welland River bridge at Merrittsville be replaced. The new bridge was to be 12 feet above the water

> so that small propellors [self-driven barges] could pass under by lowering their chimneys, with hinges constructed for that purpose, therefore saving the cost of a drawbridge.

A tender for the construction of this bridge was accepted from the firm of Cook and Berryman.

It can be assumed from the foregoing, that, by the late 1850s, a bridge and roads were in place that permitted travel with relative ease from St. Catharines to the centre of Merrittsville.

The completion of the lock at Merrittsville connecting the canal and the river, and the bridge crossing the river in the village, undoubtedly contributed jointly to Merrittsville becoming a hub of water and road transportation. And, of course, in later years, the coming of a number of railway lines to the community further enhanced the advantage and attraction of Welland as a transportation and industrial centre.

The bridge over the River Welland was to be replaced three more times. A steel bridge was constructed in the 1880s, which was replaced in 1933.

The current Niagara Street bridge was constructed in 1973.

Chapter XXVII

Minds and Souls

In the early days of Aqueduct, the population of the hamlet was not of sufficient size to warrant the establishment of a school in the community. Students were therefore required to travel some distance to the nearest township school, either in Crowland, Thorold or Pelham. As mentioned earlier in this work, there was also a schoolhouse west of Aqueduct at Brown's Bridge, near the foot of South Pelham Street.

John Price, a son of David Price, recounted in an 1897 article in the *Welland Tribune* that, in the 1830s, he attended a log schoolhouse on the north bank of the Welland River, directly across from his family home, and that the first teacher that he remembered was an American gentleman named De Vinne. Price related that, in the winter, he crossed the river to the school on the ice, and, in summer, in a canoe. However, this school was too far upstream to be considered as being in Aqueduct.

A common school (which now would be termed a public school), was eventually established at Aqueduct in 1836 in a structure called the Shotwell building, located on the north side of the Welland River near the wooden aqueduct. This pioneer hall of learning was maintained by the payment of student tuition fees.

The first actual schoolhouse in Merrittsville was a frame building constructed in 1848 at the corner of Hellems Avenue and Dorothy Street, and was called the South School. Christopher McAlpine was the first headmaster to guide Merrittsville students "along the flowery path of knowledge." McAlpine, in turn, was succeeded by Gilbert Cook, Henry Brown and Egerton Ryerson Hellems. The location of this school is depicted earlier in Fig. 23:01, on page 80.

Fig. 27:01   *The South School building, some years later.*

Higher learning in Merrittsville began in 1854, when a grammar school (today this would be called a high school) was established in a small log cabin on the property of A.J. McAlpine on River Road, near East Main Street. Again, to defray expenses, students were required to pay a subscription fee. The first teacher was Nelson Burns, who was later succeeded by James Hodgson. The school remained at this location for two years, but to provide a more central situation, was moved into the new Court House in 1856.

In 1858, the wooden building on Dorothy Street was replaced by a little red schoolhouse, constructed from Hooker bricks, and was now called the Model School. In the same year, the Reverend Charles Walker was appointed superintendent of the two schools.

From simple beginnings such as this, has evolved the education system and facilities of the City of Welland, and the Niagara South Board of Education.

Beside formal education, other cultural resources became available to Merrittsville-area residents.

Earlier in this work, it was related that a meeting was held at Brown's Bridge in November 1825 to provide for the collection of some books to begin a lending library. This meeting led to the formation of a library company, and strict rules governing the borrowing of books were laid down by the ten shareholders of the company. For example, a fine of three and three-quarters pence was levied for "tearing or folding down a leaf, or for every spot of grease." The library membership dues were seven shillings sixpence.

By the following year, the association's volumes in circulation had increased to 59, and included such works as Adam Smith's *The Wealth of Nations*, which had been published in 1776. In 1836, the site of the annual meeting of the library was changed from Brown's Bridge to O'Reilly's Bridge.

Over the next several years, the number of books held by the library company was increased by about 50 volumes annually. In 1857, it was recommemded that a *History of Canada* be purchased, along with histories of England and Ireland. These choices may have reflected the heritage of most of the settlers in the area.

But the library was not the only organization in the Merrittsville area dedicated to the cultural well-being of the residents.

A common institution of learning in the early days of Ontario was the Mechanics' Institute, whose purpose was to provide some means of extended education for adults. These institutes were sometimes referred to as "the poor man's university." In February 1858, a meeting was held in the Court House to establish such an organization in Merrittsville "for the promotion of scientific pursuits and the advancement of knowledge." A programme of twice-monthly lectures was arranged, and families and friends of members were encouraged to attend, and to use the library. The annual subscription fee was one dollar.

Merrittsville became the Village of Welland in July 1858, and the following month, the Mechanics' Institute and the Welland Library amalgamated when the Institute agreed "to receive the Books and property of the Welland Library Association.... and that the members of the Welland Library Association become life members of the Welland Mechanics' Institute." The library then moved to what was now the Village of Welland.

And thus began the Welland Public Library of today.

Another part of Merrittsville's heritage that remains to this day is the Welland County Fair, now the Niagara Regional Exhibition.

The fair has been an uninterrupted institution in the area since the Welland County Agricultural Society was founded at Coleman's Inn in Port Robinson on February 23, 1853. Such organizations were not uncommon in Upper Canada, as the first such society had been formed at Newark in 1792, with Lieutenant-Governor John Graves Simcoe as a founding patron. In 1846, an Act of Parliament provided for the formation of agricultural societies throughout the predominately rural province, to improve livestock and agricultural methods, as well as to encourage domestic farm production.

The first fair in the Niagara Peninsula was held on the farm of Ephriam Hopkins at Beaverdams, near Thorold, in 1832. Subsequent societies were soon formed in Crowland, Humberstone, Stamford and Bertie Townships.

In 1853, the Society acquired six acres of land from the Jesse Stoner farm in Merrittsville, that had been donated by a group of citizens, with the stipulation that the land be used in perpetuity for purposes of the fair. In 1857, the fair moved from Port Robinson to this Denistoun Street location, which over the years, increased in size to 15 acres.

The selection of this site at first met with considerable criticism, especially from the east end of the county, where some considered that the Merrittsville location was "too far out of the way," but this opposition eventually dwindled away.

The early fairs were strictly agricultural events, with emphasis on grain exhibitions, farm and implement displays, blacksmithing techniques and livestock reviews. Fruits, eggs, grains, cheese and butter were judged competitively. The best livestock were on display. In time, women were allowed to compete, and prizes were awarded for knitting, embroidery, breadmaking and preserving. The fair became the greatest social gathering of the year, with hundreds coming by wagon, or horse and buggy. The fair always concluded with a harness race around the oval track, followed by a picnic and a square dance.

The Welland County Fair remained on Denistoun Street for 116 years before moving to a new location on Niagara Street, near Merritt Road, and was then renamed the Niagara Regional Exhibition.

Today, the library and the fair are the longest existing reminders of Welland's early days.

If Aqueduct suffered from a lack of educational facilities, the spiritual needs of the inhabitants were no better served.

None of the established denominations conducted regular services in the settlement, and there were certainly no church buildings in Aqueduct. Rather, itinerant clergymen provided and conducted irregular and infrequent religious ministrations.

The first Presbyterian church in the Niagara area was established in Stamford village, and the minister of that congregation, Reverend Daniel Ward Eastman, began to travel through the district, conducting services. About 1848, largely through the efforts of Daniel McCaw, Rev. Eastman began to hold some services in Merrittsville on Chippawa Road, in a log house by the river, but no Presbyterian church structure was built during these early years.

The local history of the Roman Catholic Church begins in 1844 when the first priest travelled from St.Catharines to Merrittsville. Father Patrick McDonough, who was the pastor at St. Catherine's Parish from 1842 to 1850, began to say Mass in Quinn's Hotel in Merrittsville, but like most other faiths, no Catholic Church building existed in the village.

The Methodists also were served by travelling clergymen, who endured long horseback rides over bad roads, between the various log schools in which meetings frequently were held. The Reverends Egerton and William Ryerson were among the early Methodist ministers who preached in this area. Merrittsville became an appointment on a large Wesleyan Methodist circuit that included Port Robinson, Cook's Mills, Lyon's Creek and Port Colborne, but the community enjoyed no permanent Methodist church structure.

The members of the Church of England were attended by five travelling missionaries, who served through this area from 1842 on. These clergymen were sent by the Anglican Church Society, established by the Right Reverend John Strachan, the first Bishop of Toronto. The earliest Anglican missionary was James Stonham, who served a large area between Point Abino and Lowbanks. Holy Trinity Parish was established in 1857 by Reverend James Stannage, and services were held in the jury room after the Court House was erected, but the first church was not constructed until after Merrittsville became the Village of Welland.

The members of the Baptist Church hold the distinction of having the only church building existing during the days of Merrittsville, and indeed enjoyed a resident minister since 1846. Rev. S. W. Pritchard, who was the local incumbent for two years beginning in 1855, conducted a meeting in the school building on February 12, 1856, from which a petition went forth to the Baptist Association to have formal recognition extended to the local congregation. This led to construction and dedication on Church Street of the original First Baptist Church on June 15, 1856.

Fig. 27:02   *The original First Baptist Church, on Church Street, from a painting by the late Lem Hogue.*

But soon, within a few years, all the major Christian denominations had established churches in the Village of Welland.

Early records indicate that a number of burial grounds and cemeteries were located in or near Aqueduct and Merrittsville.

The burial plot of the Brown family, where John Brown and his wife were interred, is located at Brown's Bridge, on a knoll near a small creek on the west side of South Pelham Street. Today, little evidence of this burial plot remains.

Another family cemetery is located on Colbeck Drive near the Welland River, south of Webber Road, where some eight to ten members of the Price family were interred. It is believed that the first burial here was in 1842. Today, this graveyard is overgrown with weeds, bushes and small trees, and the headstones and fence have been destroyed.

The earliest public cemetery in the village was situated on Denistoun Street, at the foot of Mill Street. Some sources indicate that this burial ground was on the original Gonder farm (later the Stoner farm), and that the earliest burial took place here in 1813. In 1965, during the excavation for a watermain, the headstone of David Price was unearthed on the site of the Denistoun Street graveyard. Price, who died on February 26, 1841, was married to Margaret Gonder. Some years later, a Methodist Episcopal Church was erected on the grounds of the cemetery, and burials continued to take place for many years. Today, six homes are located on the site of this burial ground. It has been suggested that those who rested in the Denistoun plot were moved to the Anglican cemetery on Smith Street, but this report cannot be confirmed. It may well be that Mill Street was never extended through to Denistoun Street since authorities were aware of the significance of the site.

On January 8, 1859, six months after Merrittsville became the Village of Welland, the Church of England Diocese of Toronto purchased from Truman Raymond of Welland, a one-acre plot of land on Smith Street, for the sum of $170, for a "Church and Church Yard and Burial Ground." Soon after, the original Holy Trinity Church was erected in the churchyard, and the first service was conducted on July 17, 1859.

Chapter XXVIII

Local Government

Local government did not come quickly to Upper Canada. This was partially due to the small and scattered population, but perhaps more significantly, many in authority in the province, mindful of the recent American Revolution, considered that too much power placed in the hands of the population of the colonies had a great bearing on events that led to the rebellion. Lt.-Gov. John Graves Simcoe held a profound belief in the necessity for order and authority in human affairs, and carried an intense abhorrence of democracy and all its works.

Effective power was held by a ruling clique that became known as the Family Compact, and opposition to this oligarchy eventually brought about the Upper Canada Rebellion of 1837-38, led mainly by William Lyon Mackenzie.

Nevertheless, the first provision for local government in what is now Ontario was made by an Ordinance in 1785, under which a number of Loyalist and former officers were appointed Justices of the Peace and given limited civil and judicial authority. At that time, present-day southern Ontario was included in the District of Montreal, which in turn was part of the Province of Quebec, the successor to New France.

The earliest organized divisions of land in Upper Canada were the townships, which were set up and named by Lord Dorchester in 1787. The townships, however, played no role in local government.

In 1788, the District of Montreal was divided into four smaller districts named Lunenburg, Mecklenburg, Nassau and Hesse. The Niagara Peninsula was part of the District of Nassau, which extended from near Long Point to the Bay of Quinte. The main function of the districts was law enforcement, under the authority of appointed magistrates. Each district established a court, which appointed justices of the peace, judges, sheriffs, coroners and other officials. For many years, the courts were the only form of local government, and their responsibilies included such diverse matters as determining which animals could run at large, who could hold a tavern licence, and establishing what work was to be done on roads.

Under the Constitution Act of 1791, the British Government decided to revamp most of the colonial system which had been set up under the Quebec Act, and the old Province of Quebec was divided into two provinces, Upper and Lower Canada, corresponding roughly to today's southern Ontario and southern Quebec.

The following year, Lt.-Gov. Simcoe organized the four districts into 19 counties. The counties fronted on the St. Lawrence River and Lakes Ontario and Erie, and were primarily electoral ridings for the new provincial legislature, rather than being units of local government.

In 1793, Simcoe authorized a limited form of town meeting. Magistrates were allowed to call assemblies at which minor township officers were elected by the local property holders.

But significant change did not occur until after the 1837 rebellions in Upper and Lower Canada. In 1841, the District Councils Act was passed, which provided for the administration of local government by elected officers rather than by the appointed magistrates. The district councils could pass laws respecting roads, bridges and public buildings, the establishment and support of schools, and the administration of justice. However, no person was eligible for election to a district council unless he owned real estate valued in excess of £300.

The District of Niagara consisted of 22 townships, comprising the combined Counties of Lincoln, Welland and part of Haldimand. From 1841 to 1851, the municipal affairs of the peninsula were managed by the 28-member Niagara District Council. These members were chosen by the township councils from amongst their members and for the most part, the council functioned quite satisfactorily.

The first warden of the Niagara District Council was David Thorburn of Queenston, and meetings were held in Niagara (Niagara-on-the-Lake). But as the population increased, it was evident that a journey from the southern and western parts of the peninsula to Niagara could be a major undertaking for many, especially since the roads were not good, even at the best of times. But not only were council members adversely affected by the difficult travel conditions. For ordinary citizens, the long trek to Niagara was a severe hardship for those who were required to appear in court, to serve as jurors, or to attend the district Registry Office to record mortgages or deeds.

It was time for a change.

Part Five

The Village Of Welland

Chapter XXIX

Welland County

It was becoming increasingly apparent that municipal business could be conducted more expediently if an administrative unit smaller in area than the District of Niagara could be formed. To that end, the people in the southern part of the peninsula began about 1850-51 to agitate for a separate organization of local government.

On August 22, 1841, legislation was passed that reunited Upper and Lower Canada into the Province of Canada. Upper Canada became Canada West, and Lower Canada was now Canada East. The act also provided for the formation, after February 1, 1852, of a number of new counties, including Welland County, and also for "the naming a place within such county for a county town." In the interim, the legislation established the United Counties of Lincoln and Welland, stipulated that this union would later be separated, and that until such separation came about, a Provisional Council for Welland County was to be set up. The first meeting of this new council was to be held in the yet-to-be appointed county town. Finally, it was stipulated that after the Court House and Jail were erected and completed at the county town, the government would proclaim the dissolution of the United Counties.

The Municpal Act of 1851 provided that the County of Welland comprise the eight townships of Pelham, Thorold, Crowland, Wainfleet, Humberstone, Stamford, Bertie and Willoughby. It laid a heavy load of responsibility on local politicians, since these members of the Niagara District Council had to continue to serve on that body, as well as organize the new County of Welland, and also carry on the local affairs that had previously been accomplished at Niagara. This dual role carried on for about five years, while provision was being be made for the construction of the county buildings.

Dr. John Frazer, who was the Member of Parliament for Welland, and perhaps the leading figure in the public life of Merrittsville, was named the Provisional Warden of the Provisional Council of Welland County.

CHAPTER XXX

THE BIRTH OF WELLAND

An early task was the selection of a county seat. This decision created considerable dispute as different communities vied for the appointment. Various claims were put forth. Cook's Mills was an ambitious hamlet and argued that it was the geographic center of the county. Fonthill extolled its natural beauty, and was the site of the area's newspaper, the *Welland Herald*. Port Robinson was then the busiest community in the county, as well as an important canal town with docks, a custom house, and a thriving shipbuilding industry, and initally was awarded the site. The *St.Catharines Journal* of January 29, 1852 refers to "recent movements separating Welland [County] from Lincoln [County] and making Port Robinson the County Town." Local legend tells that the cornerstone for the county building was actually laid in Port Robinson at Ramsden's Point on the Clark property, but the authenticity of this tale cannot be confirmed.

In 1854, John Hellems headed a group that petitioned the Council of the United Counties that Merrittsville be incorporated as a self-governing village, distinct and separate from Thorold and Crowland Townships. Hellem's request was dismissed by the council on the grounds that his petition did not give the number of residents or the proposed boundaries of the village. As it turned out, such status for Merrittsville had to await another four years.

Finally, on April 21, 1856, an act of parliament authorized the separation of the County of Welland from Lincoln County, and declared Merrittsville to be the county town, although it is likely that this decision was made some years earlier. This appointment may have been decided because of the village's location at the junction of the Chippawa Creek and the Welland Canal. Another factor was that Dr. Frazer, the local Member of Parliament, believed that one day a railway would be built across Canadian soil between Buffalo and Detroit, and the shortest route would be through Merrittsville.

Nevertheless, the separation of the two counties did not go unopposed. In May 1855, the Council of the United Counties petitioned the Legislative Assembly to pass an act permanently retaining the Counties of Lincoln and Welland as a united entity, and that Niagara remain as the county town, or if a more central location should be desired, then the county seat be moved to Thorold. The petition also asked for the repeal of all by-laws that had been passed by the Provisional Council of Welland County.

But little was accomplished by this petition and the final separation of the counties occured on May 12, 1856, after the authorities were satisfied that the county buildings were complete.

Lorenzo D. Raymond became the first Clerk of the Peace for the County of Welland, and was appointed the initial County Attorney. In 1857, Hervey W. Price was declared the first County Judge, and Robert Hobson became the Sherriff of the new county.

The contract for building the Court House and County Jail was awarded to the local firm of Hellems and Bald, whose principals were prominent citizens John Hellems and William A. Bald. The architect for the project was Kivas Tully, of Toronto. On July 6, 1855, the cornerstone was laid by Dr. Frazer, with Duncan McFarland serving as master of ceremonies for the day. The official party collected in front of Barney's Inn on (East) Main Street, and led by the Port Robinson Brass Band, walked to the site of the partially completed Court House. The account of the day is continued by the *Welland Herald*, published in Fonthill:

> Upon arriving at the county town, we found the Port Robinson Brass Band already on the spot, and a company of local artillery.... stationed near the new buildings; also several hundred people gathered together from the surrounding country to witness a ceremony they had long anxiously awaited to be spectators of.

The official party passed up a temporary staircase to the main floor, where the cornerstone was raised and fitted into place by workmen, after which the warden deposited into its cavity a sealed vase containing coins and newspapers. On the front of the stone, a brass plate was fitted which commemorated the occasion. The proceedings concluded with three cheers for the Queen, a Royal Salute from the artillery, the rendition of *Rule Britannia* by the brass band, and suitable words from Dr. Frazer.

Over the years, the metal plate on the cornerstone has disappeared, but a close examination will reveal the location of the stone, near the south side of the main entrance to the building.

The first session of the Welland County Council was held in the Court House on Monday, August 18, 1856. The final construction costs of the massive stone structure were in excess of $100,000, including an expenditure of £25 to one Michael Quin for carving the tablet that remains to this day above the main entrance to the building. This tablet, shown in Fig. 30:02, lists the names of the 1856 Welland County councillors, but it is noticeable that one of these names has been chipped off the tablet. It has been reported by the *Welland Tribune* that this councillor was later convicted of a capital crime, and subsequently hanged on the county jail gallows, thus causing his name to be removed from the tablet and posterity.

Fig. 30:02   *The missing councillor.*

On July 24, 1858, the Village of Merrittsville was incorporated by an Act of Parliament, and was authorized to conduct business under the name of the Municipality of the Village of Welland.

This Act of Incorporation reads as follows:

> An Act to Incorporate the Village of Welland in the County of Welland.
>
> *[Assented to 24th July, 1858.]*
>
> Whereas the inhabitants of the village heretofore known as the Village of Merrittsville have by their petition represented, that the said village contains more than seven hundred and fifty inhabitants, and prayed that the said village may be incorporated as the Village of Welland; And whereas the same was duly represented by petition to His Excellency the Governor in Council praying for the issuing of a proclamation declaring the said village to be an incorporated village as the statute provides; but owing to the dissolution of Parliament and other causes, it could not be accomplished in time to take effect before the municipal elections held in January last; And whereas it is right that the prayer of the said petition should be granted: Therefore, Her Majesty, by and with the advice and consent of the Legislative Council and Assembly of Canada, enacts as follows:
>
> 1. From and after the passing of this Act, the inhabitants of the village heretofore known as the Village of Merrittsville, shall be a body corporate apart from the Townships of Crowland and Thorold, in which the said village is situate, and as such shall have perpetual succession and a common seal, with such powers and privileges as are now or shall hereafter conferred on incorporated villages in Upper Canada; and the powers of such corporation shall be exercised by and through and in the name of the

Municipality of the Village of Welland.

[*Etc., etc.*]

The second section of the Act laid out and described the boundaries and territory of the village. These 1858 boundaries are overlaid upon the accompanying map of the Welland of today.

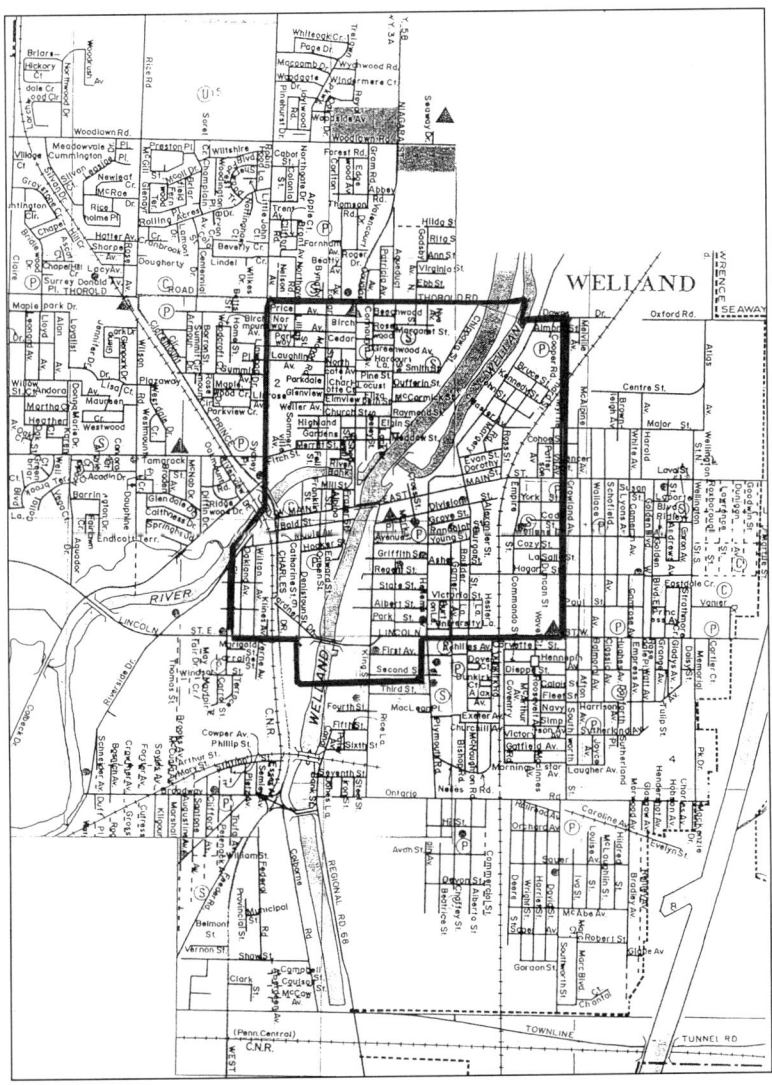

Fig. 30:03   *The boundaries of the Village of Welland, 1858.*

On August 17, Lorenzo D. Raymond was appointed the first returning officer for a municipal election in Welland, and the election was held on September 16, 1858.

The initial village councillors elected were William A. Bald, Moses Betts, Chester Demeray, Nathan T. Fitch, and Daniel McCaw. Egerton R. Hellems, who we have already seen in the role of teacher, had been appointed clerk of the village upon its incorporation, and Enoch Shrigley became the municipal treasurer. Today, the names of streets in Welland commemorate many of these early prominent officials.

The first council meeting was held in the Grand Jury Room of the Court House on September 27, 1858, at which time Daniel McCaw was chosen by his fellow councillors to serve as the first reeve of the village.

Councillor Fitch tried unsuccessfully at that first meeting to be elected reeve. He also attempted to have an individual named O'Reilly appointed clerk, but was again outvoted by his fellow councillors. Two defeats must have been too much for Fitch, since he resigned his seat on council at the next meeting, thus establishing for himself the dubious distinction of having the shortest time in office of any public official in the history of Welland. A.K. Scholfield was then elected to fill the vacancy caused by the departure of Fitch.

And so, 29 years after being founded as a shantytown called Aqueduct, and after 14 years as Merrittsville, the Village of Welland came into being. After the erection of the county buildings, the community began to prosper, and soon outstripped in importance all the other places in the county.

The small village could look forward to many years of growth and change. In the 1870s and '80s, the Third Welland Canal was constructed, only to be replaced half a century later by the engineering marvel of the Welland Ship Canal. In 1905, the Plymouth Cordage Company, from Plymouth, Massachusetts, located its Canadian operation in Welland, and the change from an agricultural town to an industrial centre was under way. The demand for labour for these industries brought great change to the ethnic mix of the city's population. The two World Wars and the intervening Great Depression of the 1930s had a profound effect on the social fabric of the community. And finally, in 1972, the Welland Canal was relocated away from the centre of the city, in effect, bringing to an end, the close relationship between the waterway and the community.

Perhaps, at some future time, this continuing story of the City of Welland may be told.

-30-

Epilogue

A moot question is why the decision was made by the Welland Canal Company to have the First Welland Canal cross the Welland River, and thus locate the original aqueduct, in what is now, central Welland.

The river has two east-west arms, one upstream or west of Welland, and the other between Port Robinson and Chippawa. These two arms are connected by the north-south channel of the river between Welland and Port Robinson.

Conceivably, the Feeder could have been carried on from the Welland South area to the vicinity of today's Dorothy Street, and there turned north, to continue on the **EAST** side of the river. It follows then, that the Feeder would have crossed the river at Port Robinson, and the aqueduct would then have been constructed at that location.

Should this scenario have transpired, there would have been no construction settlement develop near Helm's Creek, there would have been no hamlet called Aqueduct, no village named Merrittsville, and ultimately, no City of Welland.

Appendix "A"

The urban growth of Merrittsville in the 1840s and 1850s is demonstrated by the following development surveys of the village.

Residents of older neighbourhoods in Welland may find of interest the location of their properties on these plans.

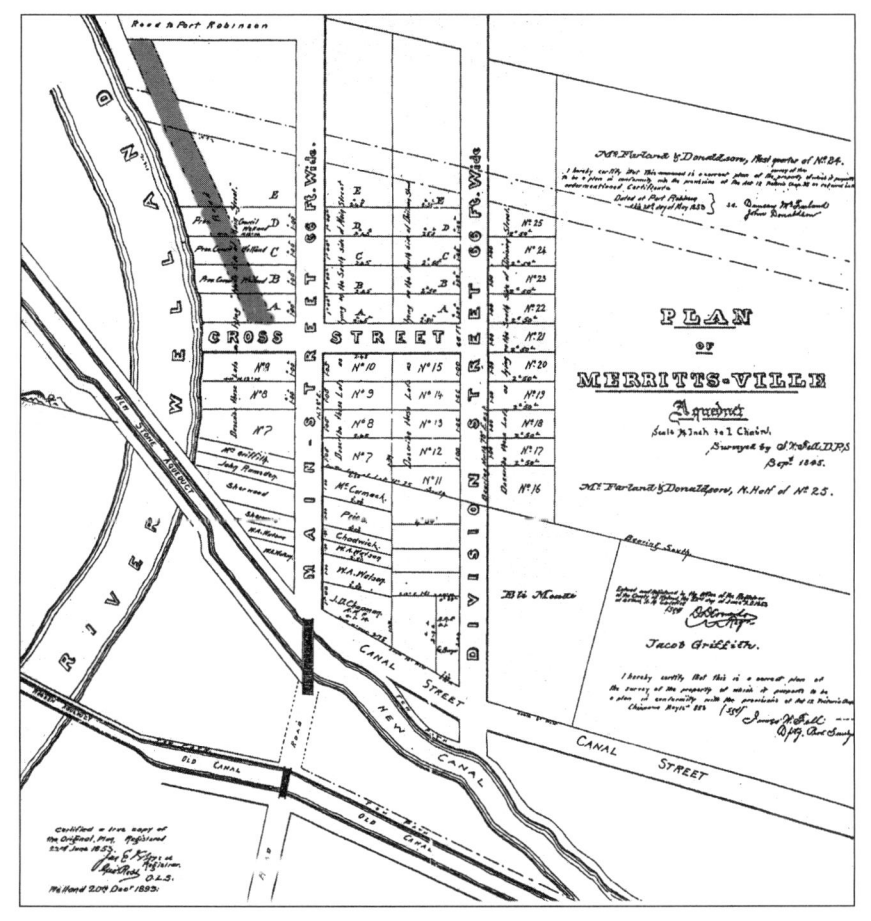

Fig. A1:01 **McFarland & Donaldson Plan**
Surveyed: September 1845.
Registered: June 22, 1853.
The original road between Aqueduct and Port Robinson is shaded in gray on this oldest plan of Merrittsville. Also depicted are the first and second canals, and aqueducts and bridges.

Fig. A1:02 **James Shotwell Plan**
Surveyed: February 1853.
Registered: April 30, 1853.
The mills and warehouse of Dunlop and Seeley are shown on this plan.

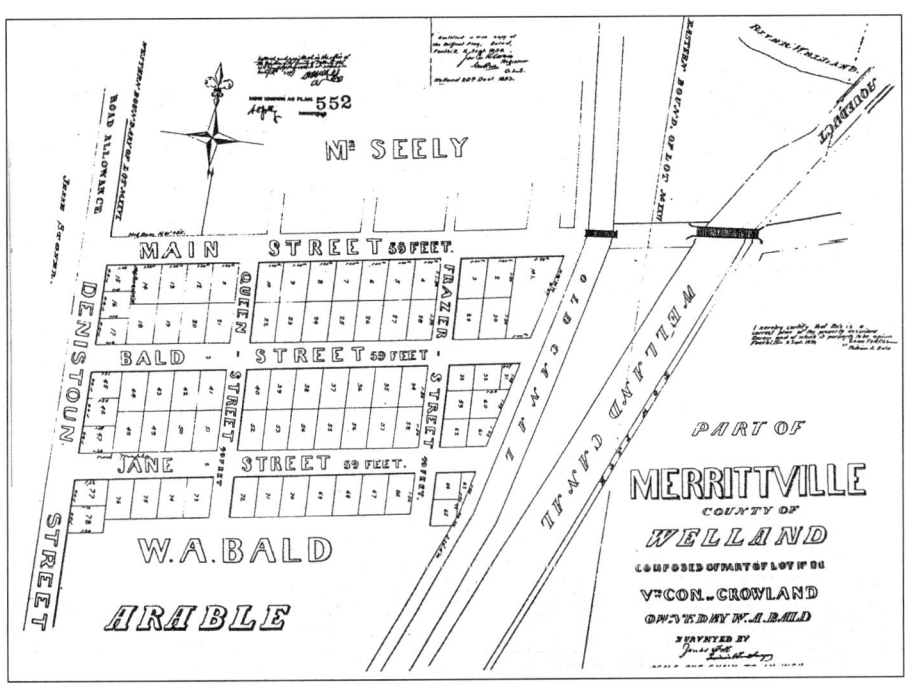

Fig. A1:03 **Willam A. Bald Plan**
Registered: September 22, 1854.

125

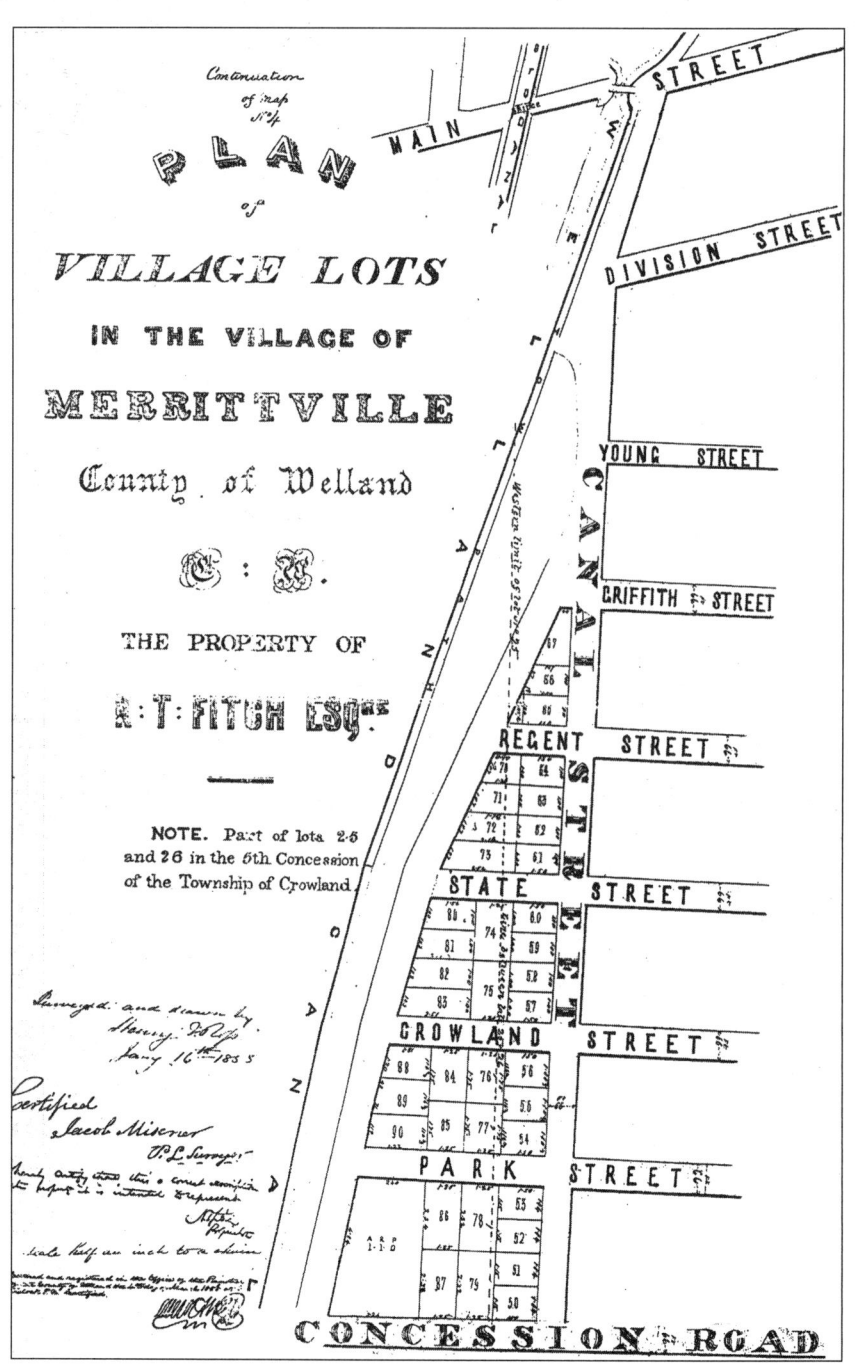

Fig. A1:04 **N.T. Fitch Plan**
Surveyed: January 16, 1855.
Note the designation C:W. (Canada West).

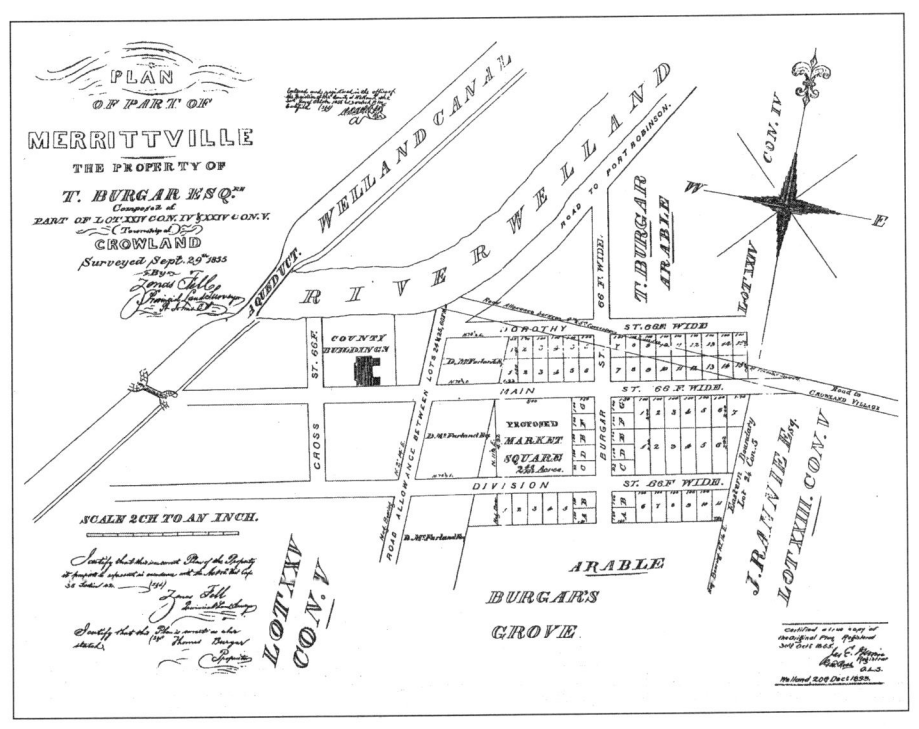

Fig. A1:05   **Thomas Burgar Plan**
*Surveyed: September 29, 1855.
Registered: October 30, 1855.
The original Main Street concession road is indicated on this plan.*

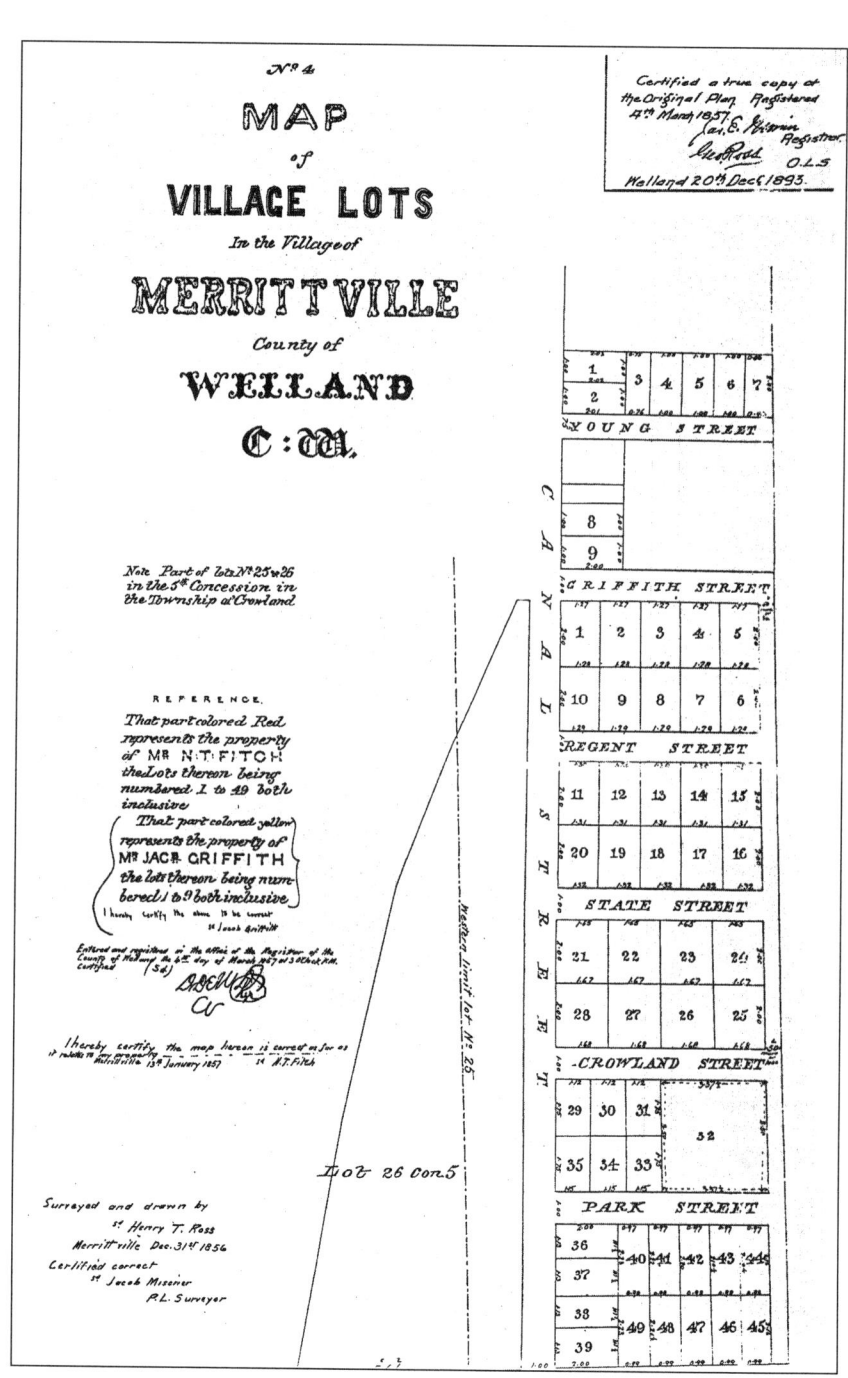

Fig. A1:06 **Fitch and Griffith Plan**
Surveyed: December 31, 1856.
Registered: March 4, 1857.

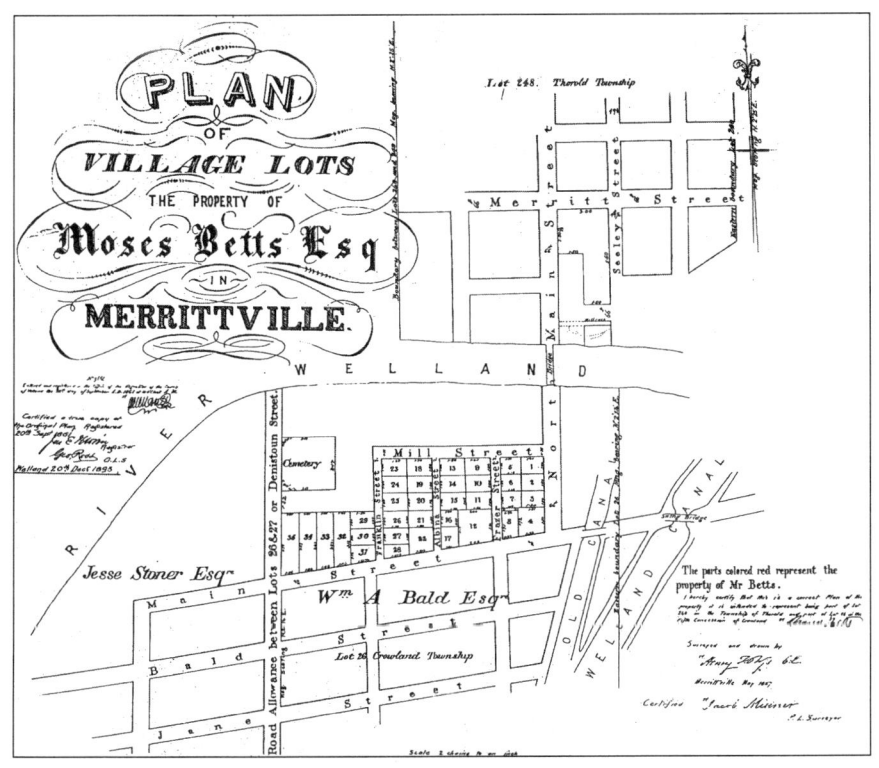

Fig. A1:07   **Moses Betts Plan**
Surveyed: May 1857.

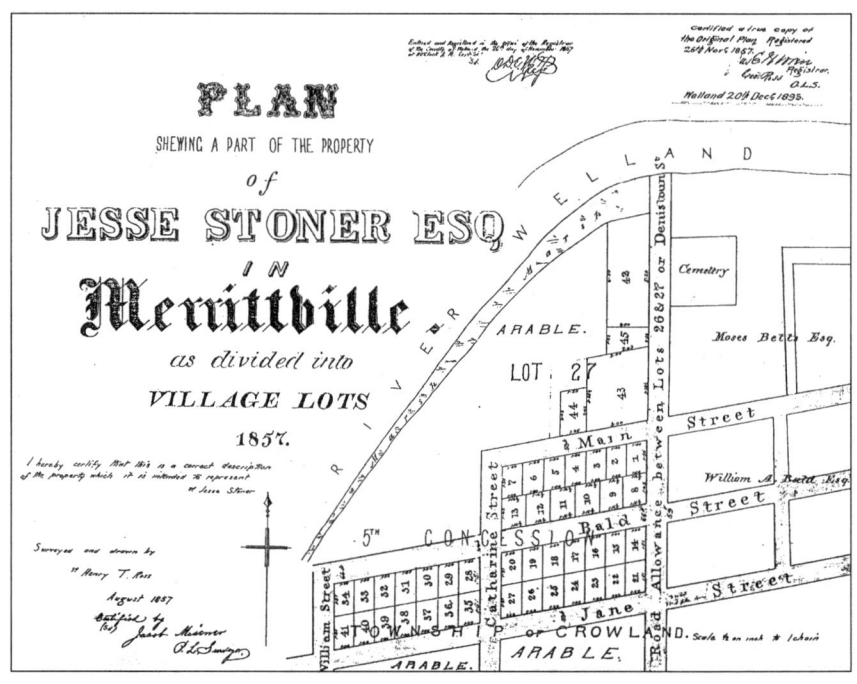

Fig. A1:08   **Jesse Stoner Plan**
Surveyed: August 1857.
Registered: November 26, 1857.
The Denistoun Street cemetery, mentioned in Chapter XXVII, is shown on both the Betts and Stoner Plans.

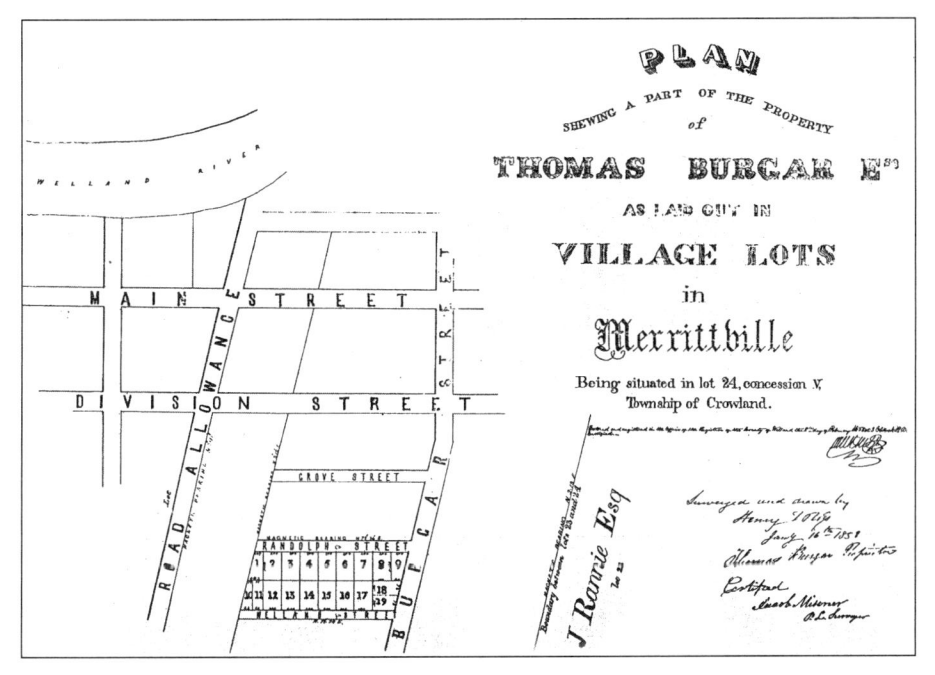

Fig. A1:09 **Thomas Burgar Plan**
*Surveyed: January 16, 1858.
Registered: February 8, 1858.*

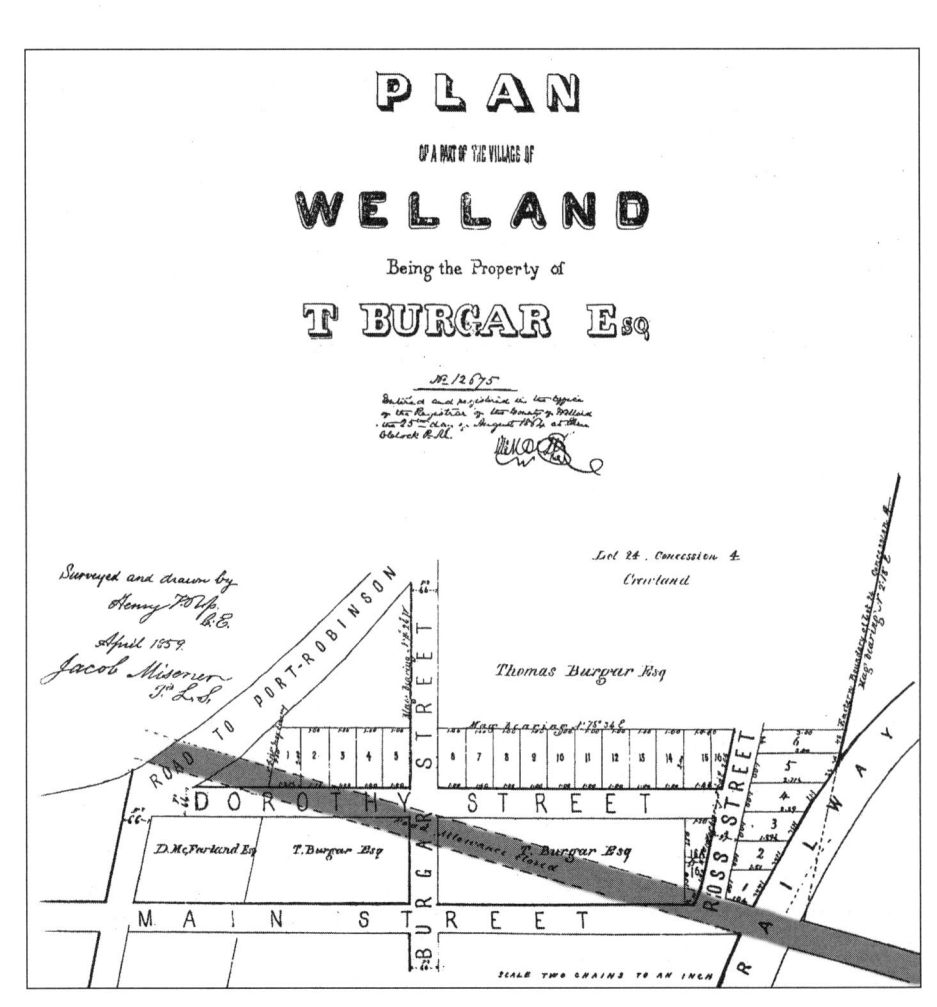

Fig. A1:10   **Thomas Burgar Plan**
Surveyed: April 1859.
Registered: August 25, 1864.
This plan was surveyed and registered after Merrittsville became Welland. The line of the original concession road from Cooks Mills to the Welland River is highlighted.

Appendix "B"

Robert W.S. Mackay's *The Canada Directory* (1851) listing for Merrittsville:

MERRITTSVILLE

A Village situated in the Township of Crowland, County of Welland, C.W. [Canada West] — distant from St. Catherine's [*sic*], 11½ miles — usual stage fare, 4 s. 3d. Population about 250.

ALPHABETICAL LIST OF PROFESSIONS, TRADES, &c.

Bald, William A., general store.
Bates, O., miller.
Burgess, Corlandt, carpenter.
Burgar, Thomas, coroner.
Cook, Moses, millowner.
Demeray, Chester, carpenter.
Disher, J. H., general store.
Dunlop & Seely, flour, saw and planing mills.
Elmwood & Mosier, clothiers.
Kennedy, -----, millowner.
McFadden, George, waggonmaker.
McCaw, Daniel, shoemaker.
McCormick, John, blacksmith.
Mead, Eli, builder.
Mitchell, John, carpenter.
Murphy, Timothy, waggonmaker.
Shrigley, A.W., general store.
Schooley, Elijah, general store.
Spears, George, miller.
Thomas, A.J., general store.
Tinney, Thomas, blacksmith.
Tupper, C.F., tailor.
Tully, P., tailor.
Wilson, John, carpenter.
Wright, James, cabinetmaker.
Yokom, Jacob, carpenter.

Appendix "C"

The complete listing for Merrittsville in *The Canada Directory for 1857-58*, published by John Lovell, is as follows:

* MERRITTSVILLE, C.W. [Canada West] — The chief Town of the County of Welland, situated on the Welland Canal, in the Townships of Crowland and Thorold. The staple article in this section of the country is wheat. Here is immense water power available for milling and manufacturing purposes. Distant from St. Cathe rines [sic] 12 miles, and from Port Colborne, on Lake Erie, 8 miles. Daily mails. Population about 800.

Anthony & Graham	carpenters.
Ayers, W.H.	foundry.
Barney, Hiram	proprietor of City hotel.
Betts, Moses	grist and saw mill.
Brown & Flynn	blacksmiths.
Burgar, Thomas	postmaster.
Burns, A.J.	M.D.
Canneff, H.	watchmaker and jeweller.
Chapman, A.	stationer.
City Hotel, Hiram Barney	proprietor.
Clump, G.	butcher.
Cummings, A.L.	clerk of Division court, and agent for Provident Life Assurance Company.
Cummings, James	warden.
Daiber, John	tailor.
D'Everardo, D.D.	clerk of county council, and registrar.
Dunn, H.	blacksmith.
Fell, Z.	provincial land surveyor.
Fitch, H.	proprietor of Welland house.
Fitch, N.T.	deputy clerk of Crown and of County court.
Glover, C.	grocer.
Goodenough, —	butcher.

Griffith & Kinsman	dealers in dry goods, hardware, groceries, produce, &c.
Hobson, Robert	sheriff.
Holmes, W.	livery stable.
Howber, Joseph	cooper.
Jarbert, V.	shoemaker.
Joiner, William	saw mill.
Lawrence, James	tailor.
Lescar, B.	butcher.
Losh, Charles	carriagemaker.
McCaw, D.	shoemaker.
McCoppan, James	general store.
McDonald, R.	stone cutter.
Page, William	general store.
Price, H.W.	judge of County court.
Pritchard, rev. S.W.	Baptist.
Provident Life Assurance Company, A.L. Cummings	agent.
Raymond, L.D.	barrister, and clerk of the peace.
Ross, H.T.	civil engineer.
Scholfield, A.K.	deputy sheriff.
Sherwood, A.	wood merchant.
Shrigley, A.W.	
Sinnett, John	mason.
Smith, J.L.	baker, confectioner and perfumer.
Spencer, V.	carpenter.
Stevenson & Adair	rectifiers.
Taylor & Harris	general store.
Thompson, William	grist mill.
Tupper, C.F.	bailiff of Division court.
Wall, N.	high bailiff.
Welland House, H. Fitch	proprietor.
Hooker, T.W.	brickmaker.

* Formerly called Aqueduct, from the aqueduct at this place by which the Welland Canal crosses the river.

SOURCES

Further information about the history of the City of Welland, the Niagara Peninsula and the Welland Canals may be found in the following sources. Many of these references were consulted in the preparation of *Aqueduct, Merrittsville and Welland.*

Hugh G.J. Aitken. *The Welland Canal Company; A Study in Canadian Enterprise.* (Cambridge, Mass.: Harvard University Press, 1954; reprinted: St. Catharines: Canadian Canal Society, 1997).

A Brief History of Welland. Compiled by Students of Plymouth Senior Public School. (Welland: 1967).

DeWitt Carter. *The Welland Canal; A History.* (Port Colborne: Privately Printed for Helen Carter, 1960).

Colin K. Duquemin. *The Historic Welland Canals.* (Fonthill: Niagara South Board of Education, St. Johns Outdoor Studies Centre, 1979).

J. Blanche Hern. *History of Crowland Township: Centennial Yearbook.* (Port Colborne: Port Colborne Citizen Press Limited, 1967).

Historical and Architectural Reflections of the Founding Peoples of Welland. By the Local Architectural Conservation Advisory Committee of the City of Welland. (Welland: 1992).

The History of the County of Welland, Ontario. (Welland: Welland Tribune Printing House, 1887; reprinted: Belleville: Mika Silk Screening Limited, 1972).

Illustrated Historical Atlas of the Counties of Lincoln & Welland, Ont. (Toronto: H.R. Page, 1876; reprinted: Port Elgin, Stratford: Cumming, 1971, 1984).

John N. Jackson. *The Four Welland Canals....* (St. Catharines: Vanwell Publishing Limited, 1988).

John N. Jackson and Fred A. Addis. *The Welland Canals; A Comprehensive Guide.* (St. Catharines: 1982).

J.P. Merritt. *Biography of the Hon. W.H. Merritt, M.P....* (St. Catharines: E.S. Leavenworth, Book and Job Printing Establishment, 1875).

David M. Michener. *The Canals at Welland.* (Welland: The Rotary Club of Welland, 1973).

G.R.T. Sawle. *Autobiography.* (Welland: 1962).

G.R.T. Sawle. *Hometown: Historical Sketches of Persons & Spicy Incidents....* (Welland: 1959).

Roberta M. Styran and Robert R. Taylor. *Mr. Merritt's Ditch; A Welland Canal Album.* (Erin: Boston Mills Press, 1992).

Roberta M. Styran and Robert R. Taylor. *The Welland Canals; The Growth of Mr. Merritt's Ditch.* (Erin: Boston Mills Press, 1988).

Souvenir of the Town of Welland.... (Welland: Welland Telegraph, Sears & Sawle, Publishers, 1902).

Welland Centennial. 1858-1958; Souvenir Booklet. (Welland: City Council, 1958).

Welland, Ontario, 1958-1983; Celebrating 125 Years of Canadian Heritage. (Welland: Welland City Council, 1983).

Illustration Credits

Credit and heartfelt thanks are due to:

• Joanne Herbert of Cantel AT&T, Toronto, for permission to reproduce the paintings of Cartier at Gaspé, Simcoe at Niagara, and the departure of the *Annie and Jane,* on pages 5, 13, and 45, respectively. These paintings were originally commissioned by the Confederation Life Association.

• Welland Public Library for pictures of:

> Hennepin at Niagara Falls, page 7,
> Second Canal Bridge, Welland, page 65,
> West Main Street Bridge, Welland, front cover and page 65,
> Morwood's Store, Welland, page 90,
> McCaw's Shoe Store, Welland, page 91,
> South School, Welland, page 97.

• Betti Michael, Port Robinson, for permission to use the illustrations on pages 14 and 15, depicting the difficulties encountered by early settlers. The sketches, by the late Rod Asselin, appeared in the *Township of Thorold, 1793-1967,* published by Thorold Township Council to commemorate the Canadian Centennial.

• Colin Duquemin, and to Bert Murphy of the St. Johns Outdoor Studies Centre of the Niagara South Board of Education, for maps on pages 37, 43 and 58, and for the illustration of the Phelps' earth-moving machine on page 39.

• Artist Fran Peacock, Fonthill, for permission to include her rendition of the first aqueduct, on page 50.

• Master Photographer Thies Bogner, of Bogner Photography and Gallery, Welland, for the photograph on page 71 of the second aqueduct, specially taken for this work.

- First Street Public School, (now école Docteur Renaud) and the Niagara South Board of Education, for the map, on page 75, of lot configurations in downtown Welland. This map is from a history of Welland, produced by the students of the school, as a Canadian Centennial project in 1967.

- Pastor Glen Barrett of First Baptist Church, Welland, for permission to use the illustration on page 102, of the original First Baptist Church. This depiction is from a painting by the late Lem Hogue, of the three Baptist Churches that have existed in Merrittsville and Welland.

- The map of early roads on page 18 is reproduced from the *History of Crowland Township: Centennial Year Book,* by J. Blanche Hern, published in 1967.

- The map on page 23 depicting the pre-canal road network in the Niagara Peninsula, is copied from "The Origins and Development of the Road Network of the Niagara Peninsula, Ontario, 1770-1851," by Andrew F. Burghardt, printed in the *Annals* of the Association of American Geographers, vol. 59, no. 3 (September 1969).

- The Merritt portrait on page 32 has been reproduced from the *Biography of the Hon. W.H. Merritt, M.P.,* by J. P. Merritt (1875).

- Advertisements on pages 38, 46, 82 and 84 are taken from contemporary St. Catharines newspapers.

- The survey plans and maps appearing on pages 52, 55 (bottom), 56, 85, 86, and 88 have been reproduced or adapted by the author, from originals in the Niagara South Land Registry Office, Welland, and from the *Welland Canal Lease Registers and Canal Surveys,* located in Special Collections, James A. Gibson Library, Brock University, St. Catharines, or from Page's *Illustrated Historical Atlas of the Counties of Lincoln & Welland, Ont.* (1876). The Land Registry office was also the source of the plan on page 89.

• The view of the Second Welland Canal aqueduct, shown on page 70, has been taken from *Picturesque Canada*, edited by George M. Grant (1883), vol. 1.

• The maps on pages 67, 80, and 83 were modified from maps appearing in Page's *Illustrated Historical Atlas of the Counties of Lincoln & Welland, Ont.* (1876). The illustration of the Welland County Court House, on page 114, is from the same source.

• The maps on pages 51, 55 (top), and 73 are original, and were specially prepared for this history by the author, as were the photographs on pages 26, 44, 66 and 115.

• Survey plans, appearing in Appendix "A", have been reproduced from originals in the Niagara South Land Registry Office.

Acknowledgements

Information on the early days of Welland is scanty and scattered. Numerous sources, organizations and individuals were consulted in the research for *Aqueduct, Merrittsville and Welland*.

I am particulary indebted to John Burtniak, Special Collections Librarian and University Archivist, Brock University, for his historical expertise, for the many, many hours that he expended in proofreading the several draft versions of this manuscript, and for his invaluable input into the physical production of this work.

Much assistance was provided by others associated with Brock University. Particular thanks are due to Dr. John N. Jackson, Professor Emeritus, Geography, for his generous input over many years. Also, I am grateful to canal historian, Dr. Roberta M. Styran, for sharing with me her intensive research of the Second Welland Canal and aqueduct.

Special recognition is due to the staff of the Reference Department of the Welland Public Library, especially Deborah Kallender, who gave unstintingly of her time and knowledge, and to Doug Abbott for his valued comments on an early draft of the manuscript.

Similar acknowledgement is due to Arden Phair, Senior Curator of Collections and the staff of the St. Catharines Historical Museum at Lock 3, as well as the Special Collections Department of the St. Catharines Public Library, and the Welland Historical Museum. Recognition is also given to officials of the St. Lawrence Seaway Authority, Niagara Region - Welland Canal, for making available to me, many years ago, early records of the Welland Canal Company.

I am grateful to Mary Severy, Acting Land Registrar and her staff, for assistance in gathering information at the Niagara South Land Registry Office, in Welland. Special thanks are also due to Marion Foley, for guiding me through the intricacies of title searching.

Further information was obtained from the National Archives of Canada in Ottawa and from the Archives of Ontario in Toronto.

Many individuals shared their knowledge of local history with me. To name a few, I give my thanks to Terry Hughes, Mary Lou Peart, Dr. Arnold Purdon and the late Lem Hogue. The assistance of Fred Farnham in obtaining information on Robert Hamilton is greatly appreciated. Thanks are also due to Hugh Pickering, of Tillsonburg, for proofreading one of the early drafts of the manuscript.

I am particularly indebted to Kristian Bogner Photography + Graphics of Welland. Kristian's artistic creativity and remarkable computer ability are reflected in the layout and design of *Aqueduct, Merritsville and Welland*.

Marjorie McPherson, of For The Love of Books, in Welland, and author Robert Foley of Niagara Falls, freely provided advice on publishing. Acknowledgment must be made also to Frank and Steve Campion, of Campion Marketing Services Ltd., to Albert Iannantuono and Patricia Faragalli of Tri-Media Marketing and Publicity Inc., and to Mike Belcastro and Wayne Hughes, all of Welland, for their valued input into the physical production of this publication.

And finally, I express my thanks and gratitude to my wife Inez, for her thoughtful input into this work, and for her endless patience during the many days and months that I was occupied with this project.

William H. Lewis,
Welland, Ontario.
October 1997.